The Gospel of Jesus

The Gospel of Jesus

According to the Jesus Seminar

Robert W. Funk, Arthur J. Dewey
& the Jesus Seminar

SECOND EDITION

POLEBRIDGE PRESS
Salem, Oregon

Cover and interior design by Robaire Ream

ISBN 978-1-59815-186-2

Library of Congress Control Number

2014947453

Contents

Acknowledgments

The genesis for a new edition of *The Gospel of Jesus* comes from the publisher of Polebridge Press, Larry Alexander, who wisely saw the need to update the original volume. The revised Scholars Translation, having recently appeared in the fourth edition of *The Complete Gospels* and *The Complete Gospel Parallels*, necessitated a complete revision of the sayings and deeds of Jesus found in this book. Moreover, the complete saga of the three stages of the Jesus Seminar needed to be sketched out, in addition to listing the full range of publications emerging from those lengthy investigations. It was also felt that the volume's critical notes could stand revision along with a better user-friendly design and typographical corrections.

Much thanks goes to Char Matejovsky for her unswerving care, excellent eye, and uncommon sensibility in the production of this volume and to Robaire Ream, an artist who brings every book he works on to an elegant level.

Ken Overberg, S.J., must be thanked, not only for his sharp editorial eye, but also for his constant interest in the historical Jesus.

Finally, I cannot forget the first editor of this volume Robert W. Funk. It was Bob's insistent and nuanced quest of the historical Jesus that ignited the labor of the Jesus Seminar. As editor of the revised edition, I hope that these revisions continue to introduce readers to the voice and vision of that disturbing artisan of words.

—Arthur J. Dewey
August 2014

The Jesus Seminar
An Overview

In 1985 Robert Funk invited around thirty New
Testament scholars to join with him in renewing the
quest for the historical Jesus. A number of break-
throughs had been recently made in regard to a more
nuanced understanding of parables. Moreover, recent
archeological discoveries had deepened the scope of
biblical scholarship. The finding of the Nag Hammadi
codices in 1945 brought a collection of over fifty texts,
including the Gospel of Thomas and the Dialogue of
the Savior, to the table, while the discovery in 1946
of the Dead Sea Scrolls provided evidence of the
remarkable diversity of voices within late Second
Temple Judaism. The full effects of the discoveries
of the Qumran scrolls and the codices from Nag
Hammadi had yet to play out in regard to the question of the historical Jesus. Upon agreeing with Funk
that this investigation was worthwhile, the group
invited interested scholars to join them.

The members of the Seminar, called Fellows, were
professional biblical scholars who taught in colleges,
universities or seminaries. The majority of Fellows
came from North America, although there were
scholars from Europe, South Africa, New Zealand
and Australia. Almost 200 scholars were involved
throughout the course of the different phases of
the Seminar. Seventy-five signed each of the two
major reports. The Seminar was never sponsored,
supervised, endorsed or funded by any academic or

religious organization. Anyone with the appropriate academic credentials could become a Fellow, regardless of religious commitments or point of view.

The work of the Seminar occurred in three major phases. From 1985 to 1991 Fellows met to consider all the words attributed to Jesus in the first three centuries. They began with an initial inventory of the data. No saying was considered out of bounds. Nor was a saying found in the New Testament canon privileged over a non-canonical saying (such as in the Gospel of Thomas).

The Fellows divided up into working groups to research the state of the question for each saying and to make the strongest case for authenticity. After each working group deliberated, their recommendations were returned to the entire Seminar which then met in plenary session to debate the sayings and to come to a vote on them. The Seminar sorted through about 1,500 versions of approximately 500 sayings ascribed to Jesus. A compendium of about 90 authentic sayings and parables was determined.

In order to facilitate their investigations, the Fellows constructed a definite protocol. They agreed to form an agenda and to come to a decision on the basis of the best knowledge at that time and in light of their best judgments. This collaborative work allowed Fellows to expand beyond an individual effort as well as to shorten the time for such intense research and argumentation. They agreed that their work was cumulative, which meant that they had to identify or form a consensus and then build on that consensus. They welcomed the broadest possible spectrum for these debates. In the course of their labor the Fellows dropped the typical posturing that usually accompanies academic discussion. A penchant for honesty and candor became a hallmark of the deliberations. The rarest thing happened in these debates—scholars actually admitted changing their minds!

From the outset the Jesus Seminar had a further purpose. Not only was this a renewal of the quest for the historical Jesus but it also became the basis of reporting the significance of this question to the public. All of the deliberations of the Seminar were held in the presence of Associate members and the findings of the Seminar were reported to the general public in order to promote literacy in biblical matters and to elevate the discourse about religion in public conversation.

From 1991 to the Spring of 1995 the second phase of the Seminar focused on the deeds of Jesus. Again a database was constructed out of any material from the first three centuries. And once again working groups determined the state of the question and made the strongest possible arguments for authenticity. Upon recommendations from the subcommittees the Fellows met in plenary session to debate, weigh, and vote on these matters. They delivered 387 reports of 176 events and deeds. Twenty-nine of the 176 events were deemed to contain historical information.

The third phase of the Seminar attempted to see what would be the possible ramifications of the Seminar's findings on the words and deeds of Jesus. From the database of the first two phases Fellows began to construct possible profiles of the historical Jesus. This debate and discussion lasted from 1995 to 1999.

Three publications emerged providing the results of the Jesus Seminar. *The Five Gospels* (1993) documents the first phase of the Seminar on the sayings of Jesus. *The Acts of Jesus* (1998) delivers the Seminar's report on the deeds and events in the life of Jesus. *Profiles of Jesus* (2002) offers a variety of synthetic attempts to detect what a profile of the historical Jesus could be.

The Gospel of Jesus graphically presents what the Fellows determined to be the authentic sayings and deeds of the historical Jesus. Readers can use this volume as basis for their own investigation into the question of the historical Jesus and for their own construction of a profile of this challenging figure.

Voting

After careful study and debate, the Fellows of the Seminar voted to express their judgments on historical questions. Voting is a traditional method among biblical scholars to determine whether or not there is a consensus and if so, what its magnitude may be. Voting was done by colored beads, the meaning of which is formulated below.

Sayings

Red: Jesus undoubtedly said this or something very like it.

Pink: Jesus probably said something like this.

Gray: Jesus did not say this, but the ideas contained in it are close to his own.

Black: Jesus did not say this; it represents the perspective or content of a later or different tradition.

Deeds

Red: The historical reliability of this information is virtually certain. It is supported by a preponderance of evidence.

Pink: This information is probably reliable. It fits well with other evidence that is verifiable.

Gray: This information is possible but unreliable. It lacks supporting evidence.

Black: This information is improbable. It does not fit verifiable evidence; it is largely or entirely fictive.

The results were an average of all the votes cast. Every vote helped determine the final color; every vote counted because the average was a weighted average.

Reporting

In *The Five Gospels* and *The Acts of Jesus* the Fellows color-coded the results of their deliberations and endeavored to give a brief account of how they reached their conclusions. Creating a color-coded report was done to make its contents immediately evident to the general reader without the necessity of reading hundreds of pages of commentary. In addition, it took as its model the red-letter editions of the New Testament widely known among readers of the Bible. *The Five Gospels* made the religion bestseller list for nine months.

The translation used is the Scholars Version, as revised and found in *The Complete Gospels*, 4th ed., and *The Complete Gospels Parallels*.

Abbreviations & References

Abbreviations

Acts	Acts of the Apostles
BCE	Before the Common Era
CE	Common Era
col.	column
1–2 Cor	1–2 Corinthians
EgerG	Egerton Gospel
epil	epilogue
Gal	Galatians
GJes	Gospel of Jesus
GNaz	Gospel of Nazoreans
GosFr 1224	Papyrus Oxyrhynchus 1224
John	Gospel of John
Luke	Gospel of Luke
Mark	Gospel of Mark
Mary	Gospel of Mary
Matt	Gospel of Matthew
prol	prologue
PsMark	Pseudo-Mark (Mark 16:9–20)
Q	Sayings in Gospel Q
Thom	Gospel of Thomas
v.	verse

References

MARK 8:1, 11–13 = Original text included in the Gospel of Jesus

Matt 16:1–4; 2:38–40; Luke 11:29–30 = Parallel texts

Cf. John 2:18; 6:30 = Related texts

Sources: Mark, Q = Independent ancient sources

The Gospel of Jesus
An Introduction

The quest for the historical Jesus

The coming of the Enlightenment issued in a profound change in the way Jesus was understood. Until that time a naïve literalism prevailed in considering the figure of Jesus. It was presumed that the different canonical gospels presented an overall coherent narrative from which the figure of Jesus could be portrayed artistically, liturgically, and imitated in ordinary life. However, when the critical question—*how do you know this is Jesus?*—was raised within the context of closely reading the canonical gospels, the quest for the historical Jesus was underway.

Critical research in the eighteenth and nineteenth centuries made it very clear that the canonical gospels contained different versions of Jesus' life and teachings. While the most obvious example is the comparison of the Gospel of John with the synoptic gospels (Matthew, Mark, Luke), even among those three gospels there are significant differences. Scholars were led to conclude that when such differences were taken seriously the canonical gospels could not be literal accounts. They are actually a blend of historical memory and the imagination of the developing community. Another way of putting this is that there were at least two different voices in each gospel: *the voice of Jesus and the voice(s) of the early Jesus community*. The search for the historical Jesus then was an attempt to hear the various voices and to distinguish them. Rather than impoverishing the gospel material, such work represented a deepening in understanding the development of the Jesus traditions.

Such critical reading of the gospels did not enjoy complete agreement; many bible readers and scholars continued to read the gospels literally. In the late nineteenth and early twentieth centuries, some joined nineteenth-century science's empiricism with a literal reading of scripture to produce what is known as Fundamentalism. Others, discounting the critical approach, embedded their literal reading of scripture within the pious practices of their denominations. Sadly some were willing to sacrifice their heads for the sake of their hearts.

The Fellows of the Jesus Seminar worked within the historical-critical tradition. They were continuing the resurgence in New Testament studies since World War II that focused on the historical Jesus, especially the parables. Further, the Fellows were quite cognizant of the historical differences between the first-century world and theirs. In order to detect the historical Jesus they had to recognize that the echo chamber of the oral world in which Jesus operated was vastly different from the print and electronic culture of their time. It was sobering to realize that, in this ancient oral culture, the primary way a person's words were maintained and transmitted was through the memory and voices of the people who remembered those words. Fellows were also quite aware that the evidence they investigated was quite fragmentary. Moreover, the burden of proof rests on those who would claim that this saying or deed came from the historical Jesus. To assess the validity of any saying or deed of the historical Jesus three things must be known:

1. What evidence was examined
2. What methods were used to evaluate it
3. What were the reasons for the judgment reached about a saying or deed

Without this information it is impossible to know how a given scholar arrived at a specific judgment about the historical Jesus.

The historical Jesus is in fact a scholarly artifact. It is historical-critical scholars' best reconstruction of Jesus as he was remembered before his death, based on the historically verifiable evidence. The historical Jesus is neither "Jesus as he really was" nor "Jesus as we would wish him to be." The historical Jesus is "Jesus as best as we can know him," based on the historical evidence available to us, and evaluated according to appropriate critical historical methods.

Yet, is it not the case that a variety of historical Jesuses have appeared in the works of different scholars? Does not this variety prove that such a search for the historical Jesus is basically futile? Such an objection comes from a superficial appraisal of the research. Significant discrepancies among scholarly conclusions arise from a number of factors. First, have the scholars considered all the available evidence for the historical Jesus? Second, what methods and criteria were used and were the scholars consistent in their application? Lastly, did the scholars take into consideration the critical history and response of the scholarly community?

The Fellows of the Jesus Seminar not only covered the history of interpretation of each item attributed to Jesus in the first three centuries, but they even became particularly conscious of the assumptions they made in their interpretative analysis. They also rigorously challenged each other to be consistent in the application of method and criteria. This was not a solitary scholarly enterprise. Moreover, the full range of the material, not just selected portions, was considered. Whenever discrepancies were noted in regard to consistency of method or use of criteria, there was reconsideration, further debate and another vote. The voting produced a consensus of the Fellows.

Such a vote meant that this was the considered judgment of the Fellows, given the evidence presented and the strength of the argument at that time. The vote did not mean the end of critical discussion. If further questions were to arise certainly there would be a move to reconsider. The results of the voting were then communicated to the public in the Seminar's major publications.

Basic findings

Beyond their thorough investigation of the words and deeds of Jesus, the Fellows also considered what details about the life of Jesus they could detect. They came to the following basic facts:

1. Jesus of Nazareth was a real person.
2. Jesus was once a follower of John the Baptizer; he quit John and returned to Galilee where he began eating and drinking in profane style.
3. Jesus talked about the Empire of God in parables and aphorisms.
4. Jesus was a charismatic healer and exorcist.
5. Jesus was executed by the Romans around 30 CE.
6. Paul of Tarsus claimed the risen Jesus appeared to him ca. 34 CE.
7. It was said that the risen Jesus appeared to Simon Peter (date and locale unknown).

In reviewing the sayings and deeds that were voted as coming from the historical Jesus, the Seminar in its third phase (constructing profiles of the historical Jesus) came to appreciate that Jesus was a creative wordsmith. They concluded:

1. Jesus was an artisan of words.
2. Jesus created stories for his audience to interpret on their own.
3. The parables and aphorisms of Jesus can be said to play provocatively against the assumptions of the first-century imagination.

4. Insights from Jesus' parables and sayings provide the listener with new images of the Empire of God.
5. The Empire of God becomes discerned when the listener actively works out the parables and sayings.

Fragments of a life

The lengthy investigations of the Jesus Seminar underscored previous scholarly findings that the gospels were later interpretive constructions that included earlier materials. The nature of the evidence that was attributed to the historical Jesus made clear the impossibility of constructing a detailed biography of Jesus.

The earliest evidence for the historical Jesus can be found in the Q Gospel. In the view of many scholars, Matthew and Luke both knew of an earlier written collection of sayings. This material can be found by removing the Markan material and the special Matthaean material from Matthew and the Markan material and special Lukan material from Luke. Scholars have called what remains (much in word-for-word agreement) the Q Gospel. The discovery of the Gospel of Thomas, which overlaps about 40 percent with Q, sustains the contention that such a gospel did exist and in a literary format quite distinct from that of the later narrative gospels. The disappearance of Q was probably occasioned by the inclusion of its sayings in the more user-friendly structures of the gospels of Matthew and Luke. The very format of the Q Gospel discourages biography. It is a collection of sage sayings—such as those found in Proverbs or Sirach—of interest to a community that saw Jesus as a wise teacher and prophet. What was essential were his words of wisdom. Biographical matters, such as birth and death, were not important, nor were particulars such as marital status or age. There is no interest in what later readers would desire. The Gospel of Thomas also continues in that vein of transmitting wisdom sayings.

The Gospel of Mark not only provided a narrative structure for early sayings material and a collection of healing stories but also set the words and deeds of Jesus within the overarching shadow of his suffering, death and vindication. Mark created a breathless sketch of a short, intense, and doomed career to speak to the concerns of a community devastated by the catastrophic Jewish War. Matthew and Luke built upon and emended that Markan structure in different ways, thereby constructing new identities of Jesus for each developing community. John further re-envisioned the Jesus traditions in light of his community's idiosyncratic history. In sum, each of the gospels uses and arranges earlier materials for a later community's needs. None of the gospel writers was interested in the past for the sake of the past. What survived in the transmission of sayings and stories owed its usefulness to the later communities. We are thus left only with fragments from a life. It is sobering to ponder what was lost as the tradition developed. But, considering that this was a peasant's life that meant little to nothing from an imperial perspective, to have anything at all is quite remarkable and due to the tenacious memory of Jesus' followers.

The Gospel of Jesus then, like its ancient cousins, is yet another retelling of Jesus' story. But the difference is that this composite is a conscious selection of all the words and deeds that the Jesus Seminar has concluded to have come from the historical Jesus. Thus this collection presents a distinct angle on the question of Jesus. Because the sayings and deeds have been untangled from the later interpretive layers, readers may, for the first time, come in contact with inklings of the historical Jesus.

Readers will see that the usual framework for the career of Jesus has been greatly reduced. The Fellows found that the birth, death and post mortem stories reflected the concerns of later communities. Indeed, the overall Markan narrative structure was seen as a later construction of the writer, who embedded and reworked earlier collections of sayings and healing stories to provide meaning for the Markan community. And since Mark became a default structure for Matthew, Luke and John, it became clear that the sayings and stories that went back to the historical Jesus did not possess any such skeletal organization. Indeed, the Q Gospel and the Gospel of Thomas, both collections of sage sayings, already pointed the Fellows in that direction. Thus the body of the Gospel of Jesus presents a modified format of a collection of sage sayings and stories. The prologue and epilogue reflect what little can be ascertained regarding the origin and fate of Jesus. Even the material surrounding Jesus' execution is quite sketchy. The amended notes that immediately follow the body of the text have been increased to provide readers with pertinent background information, as well as succinctly clarifying decisions of the Seminar.

The material in *The Gospel of Jesus* was assembled primarily from two reports of the Jesus Seminar, *The Five Gospels* (1993) and *The Acts of Jesus* (1998). Both detail the issues and arguments for the authenticity of the sayings and passages. (For more on this, please see pages x–xii above.) As mentioned earlier, the Fellows reached a consensus on all the words and deeds of Jesus. Of the 1500 versions of the 500 sayings attributed to Jesus in the first three centuries, about 90 authentic sayings were found. Of the 176 events and deeds attributed to Jesus, 29 were deemed to contain historical information. All the sayings and reports on items considered probably historical (that is, red and pink sayings and reports, see above p. xii), along with a few items voted as possibly historical (that is, gray, see p. xii above) have been included. The gray (possibly historical) material included in this volume comes from those items where the consensus vote narrowly fell short of a pink weighted average and where the Fellows were almost equally divided in their interpretation of the saying or passage. For example the passage in GJ 10:1–5 ("Children in the marketplace," Luke 7:31–35) may contain a comparison used by the historical Jesus about his contemporary listeners, but the overall structure and final interpretation ("Wisdom is vindicated by her children") comes from the later Q Gospel community. Occasionally some narrative material voted as not spoken by the historical Jesus (or black) by the Fellows has been included. Thus, for example, while the account of the Baptizer's death may well convey a fictive cause for John's death (and be considered as inauthentic), both the imprisonment and execution of John are confirmed by the Jewish historian Josephus. Finally, there is also the possibility that, while a story may be judged fictive (and therefore unhistorical), it may still be a "true fiction" insofar as it catches the probable character found in other material judged to be from the historical Jesus. Thus, the "First Stone" story (GJ 7:28–36, John 8:3–11) was judged to be a fictional construction by a later community. Nevertheless it conveyed the compassionate vision found elsewhere in the sayings judged authentic.

The material is arranged by topic and type of story. Such an arrangement, as well as the assignment of heads for particular sayings, is fraught with interpretive choices. The reader is encouraged to explore what might be the possible connections in the various sections. On the other hand, the reader should be alert to the possibility that alternative groupings are quite possible. Consider the present arrangement as a starting point, not a conclusion to exploration. In catching the voice of the historical Jesus, one becomes aware that he was an oral performer who adapted his utterances to a variety of audiences. He played with their assumptions, and they played with his words in order to discover where he was going with them. His stories and sayings begot more stories and sayings. Indeed, one can see that the earliest collections of his sayings (such as the Q Gospel) reflect the continuing activity of his followers. Jesus' stories and sayings did not silence his audience; rather, the growing tradition gives evidence of their attempts to continue to transmit and share the wisdom of their experience.

Intimations of a vision

The historical Jesus was distinctive in his speech, healings and table fellowship. His actions, however, do not become clear until we detect the vision out of which he provocatively lived. There were other healers before, during and after the time of Jesus. What was Jesus doing when he touched those outside the prevailing system of economic benefits? Moreover, in a world that judged a person by the company he kept, why did Jesus develop a reputation for eating with just anyone? Why did he flout purity rules by advising his followers to eat whatever was set before them? Why did Jesus consider the Sabbath to be created for human beings, not the other way around?

To begin to see the full intent of these actions we need to consider the words of Jesus. A person's speech betrays his vision. Now the speech of the historical Jesus can be located within the larger tradition of Jewish wisdom. As a peasant artisan, Jesus would have been heir to an ongoing conversational stream of traditional proverbs, stories, aphorisms, and illustrations. Unlike the Jewish priestly and prophetic traditions, the wisdom tradition begins with human experience. People found what was of value as they experienced life. They then shared this experience by articulating it in proverbs, stories, aphorisms, illustrations, and parables. But they did not simply accept others' sayings without testing them in their own experience. If they found that a saying had merit, that it gave meaning to their lives, then they would continue to use it and pass it on. The basic elements of this ongoing tradition (experience, articulation, testing) would have undergirded the conversation Jesus had with his various listeners (quite probably at meals). As an oral performer, Jesus would have spent time constructing his sayings to be memorable. For, in an oral culture, what survives is that which is memorable and what is memorable is that which has been creatively formatted.

Two oral formats especially favored by the historical Jesus were aphorisms and parables. An aphorism is a pithy saying that gets into a listener's head and does damage. Such a saying undermines the assumptions of the listener. A parable is a short narrative fiction that also upends the world of the listener. Even before the work of the Jesus Seminar, scholars had shown that the allegorizing of the parables (such as Mark 4:13–20) was the work of the developing Jesus traditions. The historical Jesus did not need to spell out what he meant. Rather, he challenged his listeners to work out what he said and to see how different life became when they did so. Thus, the aphorism of the "camel and the needle's eye" (Mark 10:25) did not simply critique the wealthy; rather, even the peasant listening to this comically provocative saying would have to overcome the common assumption everyone held, namely, that wealth was a sign of God's favor. Likewise, the parable of "This man was on his way from Jerusalem" (Luke 10:30–35) was not intended as an example story (although that was how Luke later framed it), but as a shocking challenge to a Jewish audience to imagine how a Jew can fall into the hands of an enemy and come out the better for it. Indeed, as the story progresses, it creates an image of an enemy that no one would have dared to presume.

But such a presumption could well have come from someone whose imagination crossed no man's land, who declared that "God makes the sun rise on both the bad and the good, and sends rain on both the just and the unjust" (Matt 5:45). Such words flew in the face of basically held convictions. Who could imagine a God who unconditionally gives benefits to both good and bad, just and unjust? Certainly if listeners identified with the good and just, such a saying would have sounded unsettling. But for those peasants who lived lives of constant desperation, such an utterance would have meant unexpected joy. Indeed, this saying also confounds those who would wish for an apocalyptic resolution, where justice is finally served and punishment handed out. Who could imagine a God that gives benefits indiscriminately in the here and now? Where does the predictable black and white world go? Who would transgress the calculus of revenge? Indeed, there appears to be a haunting coherence with the declaration that the Empire of God "is spread out upon the earth, and people don't see it" (Thom 113). Is this why Jesus congratulated the poor that God's Empire was theirs (Luke 6:20)? Did his speech connect because he offered through his words and actions a new atmosphere in which people could live and dream? What would happen if people began to live as if God were already sovereign, as if Reality were ultimately trustworthy? Where would enemies fit into this encompassing vision? Could hardened social barriers be maintained? What would happen to those who took the advice about wild lilies and a reliable God to heart (Luke 12:27–28)? Would they finally discover "What you treasure is your heart's true measure" (Luke 12:34) means?

All these questions have been raised to illustrate where this volume can lead. The Gospel of Jesus is not meant to be the last word on the historical Jesus. But it can be the beginning of an intense, ongoing conversation. The reader has a chance to rub shoulders—perhaps for the first time—with an historical figure whose words continue to stir imaginations. Do you want to enter his unsettling company? Do you wish to discover, as his followers did, that wisdom is not something to be memorized and shelved but to be tested and creatively applied? Are you willing to work with historical fragments and uncertainties? Would you dare experiment with these provocative utterances? How would you speak to others of the atmosphere of God?

There is no guarantee where all this will go. Indeed, Jesus is no longer under the control of ecclesiastical power; the figure of Jesus has leaked out beyond the confines of past formulations. The historical Jesus, that shrewd artisan of words, may be still found among the fragments. What do you hear, what do you see, when you ask what do these words mean?

The Gospel of Jesus

Prologue

Birth, childhood & family of Jesus

Jesus was a descendant of Abraham. ²Jesus' parents were named Joseph and Mary. ³Jesus was born when Herod was king. ⁴Eight days later, when the time came to circumcise him, they gave him the name Jesus. ⁵Many in Jesus' hometown asked, "This is the carpenter, isn't it? ⁶Isn't he the son of Mary? ⁷Aren't his brothers James, Joses, Judas, and Simon? And aren't his sisters our neighbors?" ⁸Phillip tells Nathanael, "We have found Jesus, son of Joseph, from Nazareth." ⁹"From Nazareth?" Nathanael said to him. "Can anything good come from that place?" ¹⁰Then he goes home, and once again a crowd gathers, so they couldn't even have a meal. ¹¹When his relatives heard about it, they came to take him away. (You see, they thought he was out of his mind.) ¹²Jesus' family took offense at him. ¹³On his visit to Jerusalem, Paul says, "I did not meet any of the Anointed's other envoys except James, our lord's brother." ¹⁴James, Cephas and John were the reputed pillars of the movement in Jerusalem. ¹⁵The risen Jesus was seen by James.

v. 1
MATT 1:1
LUKE 3:34

v. 2
MATT 1:16
LUKE 1:27

v. 3
MATT 2:1
LUKE 1:5

v. 4
LUKE 2:21
MATT 1:25

vv. 5–7
MARK 6:3

vv. 8–9
JOHN 1:45–46

vv. 10–11
MARK 3:21

v. 12
MATT 13:57
MARK 6:3

v. 13
GAL 1:9

v. 14
GAL 2:9

v. 15
1 COR 15:7

John the Baptizer
& Jesus

A voice in the desert

So, John the Baptizer appeared in the desert calling for baptism and a change of heart that lead to forgiveness of sins. ²And everyone from the Judean countryside and all the residents of Jerusalem streamed out to him and got baptized by him in the Jordan River, admitting their sins. ³And John wore a mantle made of camel hair and had a leather belt around his waist and lived on grasshoppers and wild honey.

⁴In due course John the Baptizer appears in the Judean desert, ²calling out, "Change your ways because the empire of Heaven is arriving."

⁵So John would say to the crowds that came out to get baptized by him, "You spawn of Satan! Who warned you to flee from the impending doom? ⁶Well then, start producing fruits suitable for a change of heart, and don't even start saying to yourselves, 'We have Abraham for our father.' Let me tell you, God can raise up children for Abraham right out of these rocks! ⁷Even now the axe is aimed at the root of the trees. So every tree not producing choice fruit gets cut down and tossed into the fire."

⁸The crowds would ask him, "So what should we do?"

1:1–3
MARK 1:4–6
Matt 3:4–6
Source: Mark

1:4
MATT 3:1–2
Mark 1:15
Source: Mark

1:5–14
LUKE 3:7–15
Matt 3:7–10
Source: Q

1:15–16
MARK 1:7–8
Matt 3:11
Luke 3:16
Cf. John 1:15,
26–27
Source: Mark

1:17
MARK 1:9
Matt 3:13
Luke 3:21
Source: Mark

1:18–20
LUKE 3:18–20
Mark 1:14
Matt 4:12
Sources: Mark, Q

1:21–31
MATT 4:1–11
Luke 4:1–13
Source: Q

[9]And he would answer them, "Whoever has two shirts should share with someone who has none; whoever has food should do the same."

[10]Toll collectors also came to get baptized, and they would ask him, "Teacher, what should we do?"

[11]He told them, "Charge nothing above the official rates."

[12]Soldiers also asked him, "And what about us?"

[13]And he said to them, "No more shakedowns! No more frame-ups either! And be satisfied with your pay."

[14]The people were filled with expectation and everyone was trying to figure out whether John might be the Anointed One.

[15]And he began his proclamation by saying, "Someone more powerful than I will succeed me, whose sandal straps I am not fit to bend down and untie. [16]I've been baptizing you with water, but he will baptize you with holy spirit."

Jesus is baptized

[17]During that same period Jesus came from Nazareth, Galilee, and was baptized in the Jordan by John.

John is imprisoned

[18]And so, with many other exhortations he preached to the people. [19]But Herod the tetrarch, who had been denounced by John over the matter of Herodias, his brother's wife, [20]topped off all his other crimes by shutting John up in prison.

Jesus is tested

[21]Then Jesus was guided into the desert by the spirit to be put to the test by the devil. [22]And after he had fasted forty days and forty nights, he was famished.

[23]And the tester confronted him and said, "To prove you're God's son, order these stones to turn into bread."

²⁴He responded, "It is written, 'Human beings shall not live on bread alone, but on every word that comes from God's mouth.'"

²⁵Then the devil conducts him to the holy city, sets him on the high point of the temple, ²⁶and says to him, "To prove you're God's son, jump off; remember, it is written, 'To his heavenly messengers he will give orders about you, and with their hands they will catch you, so you won't even stub your toe on a stone.'"

²⁷Jesus said to him, "Elsewhere it is written, 'You shall not put the Lord your God to the test.'"

²⁸Again the devil takes him to a very high mountain and shows him all the empires of the world and their splendor, ²⁹and says to him, "I'll give you all these, if you will kneel down and pay homage to me."

³⁰Finally Jesus says to him, "Get out of here, Satan! Remember, it is written, 'You shall pay homage to the Lord your God, and him alone shall you revere.'"

³¹Then the devil leaves him, and heavenly messengers arrive out of nowhere and look after him.

Jesus announces God's empire

A voice in Galilee

After John was turned in, Jesus came to Galilee proclaiming God's good news. ²His message went:

2:1-2
MARK 1:14–15a
Source: Mark

Citizens of God's empire

³Congratulations, you poor!
God's empire belongs to you.
⁴Congratulations, you hungry!
You will have a feast.
⁵Congratulations, you who weep now!
You will laugh.

2:3-5
LUKE 6:20–21
Matt 5:3–4, 6
Thom 54; 69:2
Sources: Q,
Thomas

2:6-8
MARK 10:13–15
Matt 19:13–14
Luke 18:15–17
Source: Mark

Children in God's empire

⁶And they would bring children to him so he could bless them with his hands, but the disciples scolded them. ⁷Then Jesus grew indignant when he saw this and said to them, "Let the children come up to me; don't try to stop them. After all, God's empire belongs to people like these. ⁸Let me tell you, whoever doesn't welcome the empire of God the way a child would, will never set foot in <his empire>."

Dinner guests

2:9–18
LUKE 14:16–21a,
23b–24
Thom 64:1–11
Matt 22:2–13
Sources: Q,
Thomas

⁹Someone was giving a big dinner and invited many guests. ¹⁰At the dinner hour the host sent his slave to tell the guests, "Come, it's ready now." ¹¹But one by one they all began to make excuses. The first said to him, "I just bought a farm and I have to go and inspect it; please excuse me." ¹²And another said, "I just bought five pairs of oxen and I'm on my way to check them out; please excuse me." ¹³And another said, "I just got married and so I cannot attend." ¹⁴So the slave came back and reported these <excuses> to his master. ¹⁵Then the master of the house was outraged and instructed his slave, "Then go out into the roads and the country lanes, and force people to come in so my house will be filled. ¹⁸For I'm telling you, not one of those who were invited will taste my dinner."

2:19–20
THOM 20:1–4
Mark 4:30–32
Luke 13:18–19
Matt 13:31–32
Sources: Thomas,
Mark, Q

Mustard seed

2:21–22
LUKE 13:20–21
Matt 13:33
Thom 96:1–2
Sources: Q,
Thomas

¹⁹The disciples said to Jesus, "Tell us what Heaven's empire is like."

²⁰He said to them, "It's like a mustard seed. <It's> the smallest of all seeds, but when it falls on prepared soil, it produces a large branch and becomes a shelter for birds of the sky."

2:23–26
THOM 97:1–4
Source: Thomas

Leaven

²¹What does the empire of God remind me of? ²²It's like leaven that a woman took and concealed in fifty pounds of flour until it was all leavened.

Empty jar

²³The [Father's] empire is like a woman who was carrying a [jar] full of meal. ²⁴While she was walking along [a] distant road, the handle of the jar broke and the meal spilled behind her [along] the road. ²⁵She didn't know it; she hadn't noticed a problem. ²⁶When she reached her house, she put the jar down and discovered that it was empty.

Ask, seek, knock

²⁷Ask—it'll be given to you; seek—you'll find; knock—it'll be opened for you. ²⁸For everyone who asks receives; everyone who seeks finds; and for the one who knocks it is opened.

2:27-28
MATT 7:7–8
LUKE 11:9–10
Thom 2:1; 92:1;
94:1–2
Sources: Q,
Thomas

On anxieties

²⁹That's why I'm telling you: don't fret about life, what you're going to eat—or about your body, what you're going to wear. ³⁰Remember, there is more to living than food and clothing. ³¹Think about the crows: they don't plant or harvest, they don't have storerooms or barns. Yet God feeds them. You're worth a lot more than the birds! ³²Can any of you add an hour to life by fretting about it? ³³So if you can't do a little thing like that, why worry about the rest? ³⁴Think about how the lilies grow: they don't toil and they never spin. But let me tell you, even Solomon at the height of his glory was never decked out like one of them. ³⁵If God dresses up the grass in the field, which is here today and is tossed into the oven tomorrow, how much more will <God take care of> you, you with your meager trust.

2:29-35
LUKE 12:22–28
Matt 6:25–30
Thom 36:1–2
Source: Q

2:36-37
LUKE 11:2
MATT 6:9, 11
Source: Q

2:38-39
LUKE 12:6–7
Matt 10:29–31
Source: Q

2:40
LUKE 12:34
Matt 6:21
Source: Q

Request for bread

³⁶Father,
    ³⁷Provide us with the bread we need for the day.

God and sparrows

³⁸What do five sparrows cost? Five bucks? Yet not one of them is overlooked by God. ³⁹In fact, even the hairs of your head have all been counted. Don't be so timid; you're worth more than a flock of sparrows.

True value

⁴⁰What you treasure is your heart's true measure.

In the company
of Jesus

Simon Peter and Andrew,
James and John

As he was walking along by the Sea of Galilee, he spotted Simon and Andrew, Simon's brother, casting <their nets> into the sea—since they were fishermen—²and Jesus said to them, "Follow me and I'll have you fishing for people!"

³And right then and there they abandoned their nets and followed him.

⁴When he had gone a little farther, he caught sight of James, son of Zebedee, and his brother John mending their nets in the boat. ⁵And right away he called out to them as well, and they left their father Zebedee behind in the boat with the hired hands and accompanied him.

Levi

⁶As he was walking along, he caught sight of Levi, the son of Alphaeus, sitting at the toll booth, and he says to him, "Follow me."

⁷And Levi got up and followed him.

3:1–5
MARK 1:16–20
Matt 4:18–22
Source: Mark

3:6–7
MARK 2:14
Matt 9:9
Luke 5:27–28
Source: Mark

Women companions of Jesus

3:8–10
LUKE 8:1–3
Source: Luke

⁸And it came to pass soon afterward that he traveled through towns and villages, preaching and announcing the good news of the empire of God. The Twelve were with him, ⁹and also some women whom he had cured of evil spirits and diseases: Mary, the one from Magdala, from whom seven demons had departed, ¹⁰and Joanna, the wife of Chuza, Herod's steward, and Susanna, and many other women, who provided for them out of their resources.

3:11–12
LUKE 9:57–58
Matt 8:19–20
Thom 86:1–2
Sources: Q,
Thomas

3:13–14
LUKE 9:59–60
Matt 8:21–22
Source: Q

Foxes have dens

3:15
MATT 5:39
Luke 6:29
Source: Q

¹¹As they were going along the road, someone said to him, "I'll follow you wherever you go."

¹²And Jesus said to him, "Foxes have dens, and birds of the sky have nests, but the Human One has nowhere to rest his head."

3:16
MATT 5:40
Luke 6:29
Source: Q

Let the dead bury their dead

3:17
MATT 5:41
Source: Q

¹³To another he said, "Follow me."

But he said, "First, let me go and bury my father."

¹⁴Jesus said to him, "Leave it to the dead to bury their own dead; but you, go out and announce the empire of God."

Other cheek

¹⁵Don't react violently against the one who is evil; when someone slaps you on the right cheek, turn the other as well.

Coat and shirt

¹⁶If someone is determined to sue you for your shirt, let him have your coat along with it.

Second mile

¹⁷When anyone conscripts you for one mile, go along an extra mile.

Sly as snakes

[18]Be sly as snakes and as simple as pigeons.

Be on the way

[19]Get going.

Narrow door

[20]Struggle to get in through the narrow door; I'm telling you, many will try to get in, but won't be able.

Before the judge

[21]When you're about to appear with your accuser before the magistrate, do your best to settle with him on the way, or else he might drag you up before the judge, and the judge turn you over to the jailer, and the jailer throw you in prison. [22]I'm telling you, you'll never get out of there until you've paid every last cent.

3:18
THOM 39:3
MATT 10:16
Sources: Matthew, Thomas

3:19
THOMAS 42
Source: Thomas

3:20
LUKE 13:24
Matt 7:13–14
Source: Q

3:21–22
LUKE 12:58–59
Matt 5:25–26
Source: Q

Upsetting expectations

In the synagogue at Capernaum

Then they come to Capernaum, and right away on the Sabbath he went to the meeting place and started teaching. ²They were astonished at his teaching, since he would teach them on his own authority, unlike the scholars.

4:1-2
MARK 1:21-22
Matt 7:28-29
Luke 4:31-32
Source: Mark

First and last

³The last will be first and the first last.

4:3
MATT 20:16
Mark 10:31
Matt 19:30
Luke 13:30
Thom 4:2-3
Sources: Q
Thomas, Mark

Vineyard workers

⁴The empire of Heaven is like a landowner who went out first thing in the morning to hire workers for his vineyard. ⁵After agreeing with the workers for a denarius a day he sent them into his vineyard.

4:4-20
MATT 20:1-15
Source: Matthew

⁶And coming out around 9 a.m. he saw others loitering in the marketplace ⁷and he said to them, "You go into the vineyard too, and I'll pay you whatever is fair." ⁸So they went.

⁹Around noon he went out again, and at 3 p.m. he repeated the process. ¹⁰About 5 p.m. he went out and found others loitering about and says to them, "Why did you stand around here idle the whole day?"

¹¹They reply, "Because no one hired us."

4:21–22
THOM 41:1–2
Mark 4:25
Luke 8:18
Matt 13:12; 25:29
Luke 19:26
Sources: Thomas,
Mark, Q

4:23–37
MATT 25:14–28
Luke 19:12–24
Source: Q

[12]He tells them, "You go into the vineyard as well."

[13]When evening came the owner of the vineyard tells his foreman, "Call the workers and pay them their wages starting with those hired last and ending with those hired first."

[14]Those hired at 5 p.m. came up and received a denarius each. [15]Those hired first approached thinking they would receive more. But they also got a denarius apiece. [16]They took it and began to grumble against the owner: "These guys hired last worked only an hour but you have made them equal to us who did most of the work during the heat of the day."

[17]In response he said to one of them, "Friend, did I wrong you? You did agree with me for a denarius, didn't you? [18]Take what's yours and go! I choose to treat the man hired last the same as you. [19]Is there some law against my doing what I please with my own money? [20]Or are you envious because I am generous?"

Have and have not

[21]Those who have something in hand will be given more, [22]and those who have nothing will be deprived of even the little they have.

Ruthless master

[23]It's like a man going on a trip who called his slaves and turned his property over to them. [24]To the first he gave five talents' worth of silver, to the second two talents' worth, and to the third one talent's worth, to each in proportion to his ability. Then he left.

[25]The one who had received five talents' worth of silver went right out and put the money to work; he doubled his investment.

[26]The second also doubled his money.

[27]But the third, who had received the smallest amount, went out, dug a hole, and hid his master's silver.

²⁸After a long absence, the master of those slaves returned to settle accounts with them. ²⁹The first, who had received five talents' worth of silver, came and produced an additional five, with this report: "Master, you handed me five talents of silver; as you can see, I've made you five more."

³⁰His master commended him: "Well done, you competent and trustworthy slave. You've been trustworthy in a little, so I'll put you in charge of a lot. Come celebrate with your master."

³¹The one with two talents of silver also came and reported, "Master, you handed me two talents of silver; as you can see, I've made you two more."

³²His master commended him: "Well done, you competent and trustworthy slave. You've been trustworthy in a little, so I'll put you in charge of a lot. Come celebrate with your master."

³³The one who had received one talent's worth of silver also came and reported, "Master, I know that you are ruthless, reaping where you didn't sow and gathering where you didn't scatter. ³⁴Since I was afraid, I went out and buried your money in the ground. Look, here it is!"

³⁵But his master replied to him, "You incompetent and timid slave! So you knew that I reap where I didn't sow and gather where I didn't scatter, did you? ³⁶Then you should have taken my money to the bankers. Then when I returned I would have recovered what's mine, plus interest. ³⁷So take the talent away from this guy and give it to the one who has ten."

Powers at work

On the move

And rising early, while it was still very dark, he went outside and stole away to an isolated place, where he started praying. ²Then Simon and those with him hunted him down. ³When they had found him they say to him, "They're all looking for you."

⁴But he replies, "Let's go somewhere else, to the neighboring villages, so I can speak there too, since that's what I came for."

⁵So he went all around Galilee speaking in their meeting places and driving out demons.

5:1–5
MARK 1:35–39
Luke 4:42–44
Source: Mark

5:6–11
MARK 1:23–28
Luke 4:33–37
Source: Mark

Unclean demon

⁶Now right then and there in their meeting place was a person possessed by an unclean spirit, which shouted, ⁷"Jesus! What do you want with us, you Nazarene? Have you come to destroy us? I know who you are: God's holy man!"

⁸But Jesus yelled at it, "Shut up and get out of him!"

⁹Then the unclean spirit threw the man into convulsions, and it came out of him with a loud shriek. ¹⁰And they were all so amazed that they asked themselves, "What's this? A new kind of teaching backed by authority! He gives orders even to unclean spirits and they obey him!"

[11]And right away his reputation spread everywhere throughout the whole area of Galilee.

Notorious

[12]Many of them were saying, "He's possessed by a demon and out of his mind. Why pay any attention to him?"

Beelzebul controversy

[13]But some of them said, "He drives out demons with the power of Beelzebul, the head demon." [14]Others were putting him to the test by demanding a sign from heaven. [15]But he knew what they were thinking, and said to them, "Every empire divided against itself is devastated, and a house divided against a house falls. [16]If Satan is divided against himself—since you claim I drive out demons with Beelzebul's power—how will his empire endure? [17]Suppose I do drive out demons with the power of Beelzebul, then with whose power do your own people drive <them> out? That's why they will be your judges."

5:19
MARK 3:27
Matt 12:29
Luke 11:21–22
Thom 35:1–2
Sources: Mark,
Q, Thomas

Demons under the finger of God

[18]But if I drive out demons with the finger of God, then the empire of God has come for you.

Strong man

[19]No one can enter a strong man's house to plunder his belongings unless he first ties him up. Only then does he plunder his house.

Satan's fall

[20]I was watching Satan fall like lightning from heaven.

Fire on earth

[21]I have cast fire upon the world, and look, I'm guarding it until it blazes.

Greek woman's daughter

²²From there he got up and went away to the regions of Tyre. Whenever he visited a house he wanted no one to know, but he could not escape notice. ²³But right away a woman whose daughter had an unclean spirit heard about him, and came and knelt at his feet. ²⁴The woman was a Greek, by race a Phoenician from Syria, and ²⁵she started asking him to drive the demon out of her daughter. ²⁶He was saying to her, "Let the children be fed first, since it isn't good to take bread out of children's mouths and throw it to the dogs!"

²⁷But she answered him, "Sir, even the dogs under the table get to eat scraps <dropped by> children!"

²⁸Then he said to her, "For that insightful answer, be on your way, the demon has come out of your daughter."

²⁹She returned home and found the child lying on the bed and the demon gone.

Return of an unclean spirit

³⁰When an unclean spirit leaves a person, it wanders through waterless places in search of a place to rest. When it doesn't find one, it says, "I will go back to the home I left." ³¹It then returns, and finds the place swept and put in order. ³²Next, it goes out and brings back seven other spirits more vile than itself, who enter and settle in there. So that person ends up worse off than when he or she started.

5:22–29
MARK 7:24–30
Matt 15:21–28
Source: Mark

5:30–32
LUKE 11:24–26
Matt 12:43–45
Source: Q

Death of John the Baptizer

Herod beheads
John the Baptizer

King Herod heard about it—by now, Jesus' fame had spread—and people kept saying that John the Baptizer had been raised from the dead and that's why miraculous powers were at work in him. ²But others were saying that he was Elijah, and others that he was a prophet like one of the <old time> prophets.

³Earlier Herod himself had sent someone to arrest John and put him in chains in a dungeon, on account of Herodias, his brother Philip's wife, because he had married her.

⁴So Herodias nursed a grudge against him and wanted to eliminate him, but she couldn't manage it, ⁵because Herod was afraid of John.

⁶Now a festival day came, when Herod gave a banquet on his birthday for his courtiers, and his commanders, and the leading citizens of Galilee. ⁷And the daughter of Herodias came in and captivated Herod and his dinner guests by dancing. ⁸The king said to the girl, "Ask me for whatever you wish and I'll grant it to you!" ⁹Then he swore an oath to her: "I'll grant you whatever you ask for, up to half my domain!"

6:1–12
MARK 6:14-15, 17, 19-20a, 21-23, 25-27
Matt 14:1–12
Source: Mark

37

6:13-14
MATT 11:7-8
Luke 7:24-25
Thom 78:1-2
Sources: Q,
Thomas

¹⁰Right away she hurried back and made her request: "I want you to give me the head of John the Baptizer on a platter, right now!"

¹¹The king grew regretful, but because of his oaths and the dinner guests, he didn't want to refuse her. ¹²So right away the king sent for the executioner and commanded him to bring his head. And he went away and beheaded <John> in prison.

Into the desert

¹³After <John's disciples> had departed, Jesus began to talk to the crowds about John. "What did you go out to the desert to gawk at? A reed shaking in the wind? ¹⁴What did you really go out to see? A man dressed in fancy clothes? But wait! Those who wear fancy clothes are found in royal houses."

Surprising vision
& advice

Teaching by the sea

Again he went out by the sea. And, with a huge crowd gathered around him, he started teaching.

7:1
MARK 2:13
Source: Mark

Sun and rain

²God makes the sun rise on both the bad and the good, and sends rain on both the just and the unjust. As you know, the Most High is generous to the ungrateful and the evil.

7:2
MATT 5:45
LUKE 6:35
Source: Q

7:3-5
LUKE 6:27, 32-33
Matt 5:44, 46-47
Source: Q

Love of enemies

³Love your enemies, do good to those who hate you. ⁴If you love those who love you, what merit is there in that? After all, even sinners love those who love them. ⁵And if you do good to those who do good to you, what merit is there in that? After all, even sinners do as much.

7:6-13
LUKE 10:30-35
Source: Luke

Unexpected aid

⁶This man was on his way from Jerusalem down to Jericho when he fell into the hands of bandits. ⁷They stripped him, beat him, and went off, leaving him half dead. ⁸Now by coincidence a priest was going down that road; when he caught sight of him, he went out

7:14
LUKE 6:37
Matt 6:14–15
Mark 11:25
Sources: Q, Mark

7:15
MATT 6:12
Luke 11:4
Source: Q

7:16–27
MATT 18:23–34
Source: Matthew

of his way to avoid him. ⁹In the same way, when a Levite came to the place, he took one look at him and crossed the road to avoid him. ¹⁰But this Samaritan was traveling that way. ¹¹When he came to where he was and caught sight of him, his heart went out to him. He went up to him and bandaged his wounds, pouring olive oil and wine on them. ¹²He hoisted him onto his own animal, brought him to an inn, and looked after him. ¹³The next day he took out two denarii, which he gave to the innkeeper, and said, "Look after him, and on my way back I'll reimburse you for any extra expense you've had."

Reciprocity

¹⁴Forgive, and you'll be forgiven.

Forgive our debts

¹⁵Forgive our debts to the extent that we have forgiven those in debt to us.

Unforgiving debtor

¹⁶This is why the empire of Heaven should be compared to a human ruler who decided to settle accounts with his slaves. ¹⁷When the process began, this debtor was brought to him who owed a gazillion dollars. ¹⁸Since he couldn't pay it back, the ruler ordered him sold, along with his wife and children and everything he had, so he could recover his money.

¹⁹At this prospect, the slave knelt down and groveled before him: "Be patient with me and I'll pay you back in full." ²⁰Because he was compassionate, the master of that slave let him go and canceled the debt.

²¹As soon as he got out, that same slave collared one of his fellow slaves who owed him five thousand dollars, and grabbed him by the neck and demanded, 'Pay back what you owe!'

²²His fellow slave knelt down and begged him, 'Be patient with me and I'll pay you back.'

7:28-36
JOHN 8:3-11
Source: fragment
of an unknown
gospel

²³But he wasn't interested; instead, he went out and threw him in prison until he paid the debt.

²⁴When his fellow slaves realized what had happened, they were terribly upset and went and reported to their master everything that had happened.

²⁵At that point, his master summoned him. "You wicked slave," he says to him, "I canceled your entire debt because you begged me. ²⁶Wasn't it only fair for you to treat your fellow slave with the same consideration as I treated you?" ²⁷And the master was so angry he turned him over to the torturers until he paid back everything he owed.

The first stone

²⁸The scholars and Pharisees bring him a woman who was caught committing adultery. They make her stand there in front of everybody, ²⁹and they address him, "Teacher, this woman was caught in the act of adultery. ³⁰In the Law Moses commanded us to stone women like this. What do you say?" (³¹They said this to trap him, so they would have something to accuse him of.)

Jesus stooped down and began drawing on the ground with his finger. ³²When they insisted on an answer, he stood up and replied, "Whoever is sinless in this crowd should go ahead and throw the first stone at her. ³³Once again he squatted down and continued writing on the ground.

³⁴His audience began to drift away, one by one—the elders were the first to go—until Jesus was the only one left, with the woman there in front of him.

³⁵Jesus stood up and said to her, "Woman, where is everybody? Hasn't anyone condemned you?"

³⁶She replied, "No one, sir."

"I don't condemn you either," said Jesus. "You're free to go; but from now on, no more sinning."

A place at the table

Dining with sinners

It so happened that Jesus was reclining <for dinner> in his house, along with many toll collectors and sinners and Jesus' disciples. (²You see, there were many of these people and they were all following him.) ³And whenever the Pharisees' scholars saw him eating with sinners and toll collectors, they would question his disciples, "What's he doing eating with toll collectors and sinners?"

⁴When Jesus overhears, he says to them, "Since when do the able-bodied need a doctor? It's the sick who do. ⁵I did not come to enlist the upright but sinners!"

A bad reputation

⁶Now the toll collectors and sinners kept crowding around Jesus so they could hear him. ⁷But the Pharisees and the scholars would complain to each other, "This guy welcomes sinners and eats with them."

Advice for eating on the road

⁸Whenever you enter a house, first say, "Peace to this house." ⁹Stay at that one house, eating and drinking whatever they provide, for workers deserve their

8:1-5
MARK 2:15–17
Matt 9:10–13
Luke 5:29–32
GosFr 1224 5:1–2
Sources: Mark, Gospel Fragment 1224

8:6-7
LUKE 15:1–2
Source: Luke

8:8-10
LUKE 10:5, 7, 8
Mark 6:10
Luke 9:4
Matt 10:11–13
Thom 14:4
Sources: Q, Mark, Thomas

8:11–12
MARK 2:18–19
Matt 9:14–15
Luke 5:33–34
Source: Mark

wages. Do not move from house to house. [10]Whenever you enter a town and they welcome you, eat whatever they offer you.

8:13–14
THOM 47:3–4
Luke 5:37–39
Mark 2:22
Matt 9:17
Sources: Thomas,
Luke, Mark,
common lore

Question of fasting

[11]John's disciples and the Pharisees had the custom of fasting, and they come and ask him, "Why do the disciples of John fast, and the disciples of the Pharisees, but your disciples don't?"

[12]And Jesus said to them, "The groom's friends can't fast while the groom is around, can they? So long as the groom is around, you can't expect them to fast."

Aged wine

[13]Nobody drinks aged wine and immediately wants to drink new wine. [14]New wine is not poured into old wineskins, or they might break, and aged wine is not poured into a new wineskin, or it might spoil.

Jesus & purity matters

Eating with defiled hands

The Pharisees gather around him, along with some of the scholars, who had come from Jerusalem. [2]When they notice some of his disciples eating their meal with defiled hands, that is to say, without washing their hands ([3]you see, the Pharisees and the Jews never eat without first washing their hands in a particular way, always observing the tradition of the elders, [4]and they won't eat when they get back from the marketplace without washing again, and there are many other traditions they cherish, such as the washing of cups and jugs and kettles), [5]the Pharisees and the scholars start questioning him: "Why don't your disciples live up to the tradition of the elders, instead of eating bread with defiled hands?"

9:1–5
MARK 7:1–5
Source: Mark

9:6–8
MARK 7:14–16
Thom 14:5
Matt 15:10–11
Sources: Mark, Thomas

9:9–10
THOM 89:1–2
Luke 11:39–40
Matt 23:25–26
Sources: Thomas, Q

What goes in

[6]Listen to me, all of you, and try to understand. [7]What goes into you can't defile you; what comes out of you can. [8]If anyone here has two good ears, use 'em!

Inside and outside

[9]Why do you wash the outside of the cup? [10]Don't you understand that the one who made the inside is also the one who made the outside?

Celebration

Children in the marketplace

What do the people of this generation remind me of? What are they like? ²They are like children sitting in the marketplace and calling out to one another,

10:1–5
LUKE 7:31–35
Matt 11:16–19
Source: Q

> We played the flute for you,
> but you wouldn't dance;
> we sang a dirge,
> but you wouldn't weep.

10:6–7
LUKE 15:8–9
Source: Luke

³Just remember, John the Baptizer appeared on the scene, eating no bread and drinking no wine, and you say, "He's possessed." ⁴The Human One appeared on the scene both eating and drinking, and you say, "There's a glutton and a drunk, a crony of toll collectors and sinners!" ⁵Indeed, Wisdom is vindicated by all her children.

Lost coin

⁶Is there any woman with ten drachmas, who if she loses one, wouldn't light a lamp and sweep the house and search high and low until she finds it? ⁷When she finds it, she invites her friends and neighbors over and says, "Celebrate with me, because I've found the drachma I lost."

Lost sheep

10:8–10
LUKE 15:4–6
Matt 18:12–13
Thom 107:2
Sources: Q,
Thomas

[8]Is there any one of you who owns a hundred sheep and one of them gets lost, who wouldn't leave the ninety-nine in the wild and go after the one that got lost until he finds it? [9]And when he finds it, he is happy and hoists it onto his shoulders. [10]Once he gets home, he invites his friends and his neighbors over,

10:11–12
MATT 13:44
Thom 109:1–3
Sources: Matthew,
Thomas

and says to them, "Celebrate with me, because I've found my lost sheep."

Cache of coins

10:13–14
THOM 76:1–2
Matt 13:45–46
Sources: Thomas,
Matthew

[11]The empire of Heaven is like treasure hidden in a field. When someone finds it, that person covers it up again, [12]and out of sheer joy goes and sells every last possession and buys that field.

10:15–45
LUKE 15:11–32
Source: Luke

Pearl

[13]The Father's empire is like a merchant who had a supply of merchandise and then found a pearl. [14]That merchant was prudent; he sold the merchandise and bought the single pearl for himself.

A man who had two sons

[15]Once there was this man who had two sons. [16]The younger of them said to his father, "Father, give me the share of the property that's coming to me." [17]So he divided his resources between them.

[18]Not too many days later, the younger son got all his things together and left home for a faraway country, where he squandered his resources by living recklessly. [19]Just when he had spent it all, a serious famine swept through that country, and he began to do without. [20]So he went and hired himself out to one of the citizens of that country, who sent him out to his farm to feed the pigs. [21]He longed to satisfy his hunger with the carob pods, which the pigs usually ate; but no one offered him anything.

²²Coming to his senses he said, "Lots of my father's hired hands have more than enough to eat, while here I am starving to death! ²³I'll get up and go to my father and I'll say to him, 'Father, I have sinned against Heaven and against you. ²⁴I no longer deserve to be called your son; treat me like one of your hired hands.'" ²⁵And he got up and returned to his father.

²⁶But while he was still a long way off, his father caught sight of him and was moved to compassion. ²⁷He went running out to him, threw his arms around his neck, and kissed him. ²⁸And the son said to him, "Father, I have sinned against Heaven and against you. ²⁹I no longer deserve to be called your son."

³⁰But the father said to his slaves, "Hurry up! Bring out the finest robe and put it on him; put a ring on his finger and sandals on his feet. ³¹Fetch the fat calf and slaughter it; let's have a feast and celebrate, ³²because this son of mine was dead and has come back to life; he was lost and now is found." ³³And they started celebrating.

³⁴Now his elder son was out in the field; ³⁵and as he got closer to the house, he heard music and dancing. ³⁶He called one of the servant boys over and asked what was going on.

³⁷He told him, "Your brother has come home and your father has slaughtered the fat calf, because he has him back safe and sound."

³⁸But he was angry and refused to go in. ³⁹So his father came out and began to plead with him. ⁴⁰But he answered his father, "See here, all these years I have slaved for you. I never once disobeyed any of your orders; ⁴¹but you never once let me have a kid goat so I could celebrate with my friends. ⁴²But when this son of yours shows up, the one who has devoured your assets with whores—for him you slaughter the fat calf."

⁴³But <the father> said to him, "My child, you are always at my side. ⁴⁴Everything that's mine is yours.

[45]But we just had to celebrate and rejoice, because this brother of yours was dead and has come back to life; he was lost and now is found."

Sabbath observance

Master of the sabbath

It so happened that he was making his way through the grainfields on the Sabbath, and his disciples began to strip heads of grain as they made their way. ²And the Pharisees started to argue with him: "See here, why are they doing what's not permitted on the Sabbath?"

³And he says to them,

"The Sabbath was created for human beings,
not human beings for the Sabbath.

⁴ So, the Human One is master even of the Sabbath."

11:1–4
MARK 2:23–24, 27–28
Matt 12:1–2, 8
Luke 6:1–2, 5
Source: Mark

11:5–11
MARK 3:1–5
Matt 12:9–13
Luke 6:6–10
Source: Mark

Man with the crippled hand

⁵Then he went back to the meeting place, and a man with a crippled hand was there. ⁶So they kept an eye on him, to see whether he would heal the man on the Sabbath, so they could denounce him. ⁷And he says to the man with the crippled hand, "Get up here in front of everybody." ⁸Then he says to them, "On the Sabbath is it permitted to do good or to do evil, to save life or to kill?"

⁹But they remained silent. ¹⁰And looking right at them with outrage, exasperated at their closed mindedness, he says to the man, "Hold out your hand." ¹¹He held it out and his hand was restored.

Kinship in
the empire

Jesus' relatives
think him mad

Then he goes home, and once again a crowd gathers, so they couldn't even have a meal. [2]When his relatives heard about it, they came to take him away. ([3]You see, they thought he was out of his mind.)

[4]Many of them were saying, "He's possessed by a demon and out of his mind. Why pay any attention to him?"

True relatives

[5]Then his mother and his brothers arrive. While still outside, they send in and ask for him. [6]A crowd was sitting around him, and they say to him, "Look, your mother and your brothers are outside looking for you."

[7]In response he says to them, "Who are my mother and brothers?"

[8]And looking right at those seated around him in a circle, he says, "Here are my mother and my brothers. [9]Whoever does God's will, that's my brother and sister and mother."

12:1–3
MARK 3:20–21
Source: Mark

12:4
JOHN 10:20
Source: John

12:5–9
MARK 3:31–35
Matt 12:46–50
Luke 8:19–21
Thom 99:1–3
Sources: Mark, Thomas

Hating father and mother

12:10-11
LUKE 14:25-26
Matt 10:37
Thom 55:1; 101:1-2
Sources: Q,
Thomas

12:12-19
MARK 6:1-6
Matt 13:54-58
Source: Mark

¹⁰Once when hordes of people were traveling with him, he turned and addressed them: ¹¹"If any of you comes to me and does not hate your own father and mother and wife and children and brothers and sisters—yes, even your own life—you cannot be my disciple."

No respect at home

¹²Then he left that place, and he comes to his hometown, and his disciples follow him. ¹³When the Sabbath arrived, he started teaching in the meeting place; and many who heard him were astounded and said so: "Where's he getting all this?" and "Where'd he get all this wisdom?" and ¹⁴"Where'd he get the power to perform such miracles? ¹⁵This is the carpenter, isn't it? Isn't he the son of Mary? And aren't his brothers James, Joses, Judas, and Simon? And aren't his sisters our neighbors?" ¹⁶And they took offense at him.

¹⁷Jesus used to tell them, "No prophet is disrespected, except on his home turf and among his relatives and at home."

¹⁸He was unable to perform a single miracle there, except that he did cure a few by laying hands on them, though he was always shocked at their lack of trust. ¹⁹And he used to go around the villages, teaching in a circuit.

In parables

Teaching by the sea

Once again he started to teach beside the sea. ²An enormous crowd gathers around him, so he climbs into a boat and sits there on the water facing the huge crowd on the shore.

³He would then teach them many things in parables.

13:1–3
MARK 4:1–2
Matt 13:1–3
Source: Mark

Sower

⁴Listen to this! This sower went out to sow. ⁵While he was sowing, some seed fell along the path, and the birds came and devoured it. ⁶Other seed fell on rocky ground where there wasn't much soil, and it came up right away because the soil had no depth. ⁷But when the sun came up it was scorched, and because it had no root it withered. ⁸Still other seed fell among thorns, and the thorns came up and choked it, so that it produced no fruit. ⁹Finally, some seed fell on good soil and started producing fruit. The seed sprouted and grew: one part had a yield of thirty, another part sixty, and a third part one hundred.

13:4–9
MARK 4:3–8
Matt 13:3–8
Luke 8:5–8
Thom 9:1–5
Sources: Mark, Thomas

Seed and harvest

¹⁰The empire of God is like this: suppose someone sows seed on the ground, ¹¹and sleeps and rises night and day, and the seed sprouts and matures, although

13:10–13
MARK 4:26–29
Thom 21:9
Sources: Mark, Thomas

13:14–25
LUKE 16:1–8
Source: Luke

13:26–29
LUKE 18:2–5
Source: Luke

the sower is unaware of it. ¹²The earth produces fruit on its own, first a shoot, then a head, then mature grain on the head. ¹³But when the grain ripens, right away he sends for the sickle, because it's harvest time.

The dishonest manager

¹⁴There was this rich man whose manager had been maliciously accused of squandering his master's property. ¹⁵He called him in and said, "What's this I hear about you? Turn in your record books; you're no longer working here."

¹⁶Then the manager said to himself, "What am I going to do? My master is firing me. I'm not able to dig ditches and I'm ashamed to beg. ¹⁷I've got it! I know what I'll do so doors will open for me when I'm removed from management."

¹⁸So he called in each of his master's debtors. He said to the first, "How much do you owe my master?"

¹⁹He said, "Five hundred gallons of olive oil."

²⁰And he said to him, "Here is your invoice; sit down right now and make it two hundred and fifty."

²¹Then he said to another, "And how much do you owe?"

²²He said, "A thousand bushels of wheat."

²³He says to him, "Here is your invoice; make it eight hundred."

²⁴The master praised the dishonest manager because he had acted prudently.

²⁵For the children of this world are more prudent in dealing with their own kind than are the children of light.

Corrupt judge

²⁶Once there was a judge in this town who neither feared God nor had any respect for people.

²⁷In that same town was a widow who kept coming to him and demanding, "Give me a ruling against my opponent."

²⁸For a while he refused; but eventually he said to himself, "I don't fear God and I have no respect for people, ²⁹but this widow keeps pestering me. So I'm going to rule in her favor, or else she'll keep coming back until she wears me down."

13:30-36
THOM 65:1-7
Mark 12:1-8
Matt 21:33-39
Luke 20:9-15
Sources: Thomas, Mark

Leased vineyard

13:37-39
THOM 98:1-3
Source: Thomas

³⁰A [greedy] man owned a vineyard and rented it to some farmers, so they could work it and he could collect its crop from them.

³¹He sent his slave so the farmers would give him the vineyard's crop. ³²They grabbed him, beat him, and almost killed him, and the slave returned and told his master.

³³His master said, "Perhaps he didn't know them."

³⁴He sent another slave, and the farmers beat that one as well.

³⁵Then the master sent his son and said, "Perhaps they'll show my son some respect."

³⁶Because the farmers knew that he was the heir to the vineyard, they grabbed him and killed him.

The assassin

³⁷The Father's empire is like someone who wanted to kill a strong man. ³⁸While still at home he drew his sword and thrust it into the wall to find out whether his hand would be strong enough. ³⁹Then he killed the strong man.

Public &
private piety

Closet prayer

When you pray, go into a room by yourself and shut the door behind you.

14:1
MATT 6:6
Source: Matthew

Divine address

14:2–4
LUKE 11:2
Matt 6:9
Source: Q

[2]When you pray, you should say:
[3]"Father, your name be revered.
[4]Your empire be established."

14:5–9
LUKE 18:10–14
Source: Luke

Pharisee and toll collector

[5]Two men went up to the temple to pray, one a Pharisee and the other a toll collector.

[6]The Pharisee stood off by himself and prayed as follows: "I thank you, God, that I'm not like everybody else, thieving, unjust, adulterous, and especially not like that toll collector over there. [7]I fast twice a week; I donate ten percent of everything that I acquire."

[8]But the toll collector stood at a distance at a distance and didn't even dare to look up, but struck his chest, saying, "God, have mercy on me, sinner that I am."

[9]Let me tell you, the second man went back home vindicated but the first one did not. For those who

14:10-11
THOM 26:1-2
Matt 7:3-5
Luke 6:41-42
Sources: Thomas,
Q

promote themselves will be demoted, but those who demote themselves will be promoted.

Sliver and timber

14:12
LUKE 12:2
Matt 10:26b
Thom 5:2, 6:5
Luke 8:17
Mark 4:22
Sources: Thomas,
Q, Mark

[10]Jesus said, "You see the sliver in your friend's eye, but you don't see the timber in your own eye. [11]When you take the timber out of your own eye, then you will see well enough to remove the sliver from your friend's eye."

Veiled and unveiled

14:13
LUKE 20:46
Mark 12:38-39
Luke 11:43
Matt 23:5-7
Sources: Mark, Q

[12]There is nothing covered up that won't be exposed, or hidden that won't be made known.

Scholars' privileges

14:14
MATT 6:3
Thom 62:2
Sources: Matthew,
Thomas

[13]Be on guard against the scholars who like to parade around in long robes, and who love respectful greetings in the marketplaces and the prominent seats in the synagogues and the best couches at banquets.

Left and right hands

[14]When you give to charity, don't let your left hand in on what your right hand is up to.

Signs of
God's empire

Demand for a sign

The Pharisees came out and started to argue with him. To put him to the test, they demanded a sign from heaven. ²He groaned under his breath and says, "Why does this generation demand a sign? Let me tell you, this generation won't get any sign!"

³And turning his back on them, he got back in the boat and crossed over to the other side.

15:1–3
MARK 8:11–13
Matt 16:1–4;
12:38–40;
Luke 11:29–30
Cf. John 2:18; 6:30
Sources: Mark, Q

The presence of God's empire

⁴When will the <Father's> empire come?

⁵It won't come by watching for it. ⁶It won't be said, "Look, here!" or "Look, there!" ⁷Rather, the Father's empire is spread out upon the earth, and people don't see it.

⁸You won't be able to observe the coming of the empire of God. ⁹People won't be able to say, "Look, here it is!" or "Over there!" ¹⁰On the contrary, the empire of God is among you.

15:4–7
THOM 113:1–4
Source: Thomas

15:8–10
LUKE 17:20–21
Source: Q

15:11
LUKE 11:2
Matt 6:10
Source: Q

Establish your empire

¹¹Father, your name be revered.
    Your empire be established.

Six healings

Peter's mother-in-law

And when Jesus came to Peter's house, he noticed his mother-in-law lying sick with a fever. ²He touched her hand and the fever disappeared. Then she got up and started looking after him.

Leper

³Then a leper comes up to him, pleads with him, falls down on his knees, and says to him, "If you want to, you can make me clean."

⁴Although Jesus was indignant, he stretched out his hand, touched him, and says to him, "Okay—you're clean!"

⁵And right away the leprosy disappeared, and he was made clean.

Paralytic and four carriers

⁶Some days later he went back to Capernaum and was rumored to be at home. ⁷And many people crowded around so there was no longer any room, even outside the door. Then he started speaking to them. ⁸Some people then show up with a paralytic being carried by four of them. ⁹And when they couldn't get near him because of the crowd, they removed the roof above him. After digging it out, they lowered the mat on

16:1–2
MATT 8:14–15
Mark 1:29–31
Luke 4:38–39
Source: Mark

16:3–5
MARK 1:40–42
Matt 8:1–3
Luke 5:12–13
EgerG 2:1–3
Sources: Mark,
Egerton Gospel

16:6–12
MARK 2:1–5a,
11–12
Matt 9:1–2a, 6b–8
*Luke 5:17–20a,
24b–26*
Source: Mark

16:13–16
MARK 5:24–25,
27, 29
Matt 9:19–20
Luke 8:43–44
Source: Mark

16:17–20
MARK 8:22–25
John 9:1, 5–7
Source: Mark

16:21–27
MARK 10:46–52
Matt 20:29–34
Luke 18:35–43
Source: Mark

which the paralytic was lying. [10]When Jesus noticed their trust, he says to the paralytic, [11]"Get up, pick up your mat and walk!" [12]And he got up, picked his mat right up, and walked out as everyone looked on. So they all became ecstatic, extolled God, and exclaimed, "We've never seen the likes of this!"

Woman with a chronic flow of blood

[13]A large crowd started following and shoving against him. [14]And there was a woman who had experienced a chronic flow of blood for twelve years. [15]When she heard about Jesus, she came up from behind in the crowd and touched his cloak. [16]And right away her flow of blood stopped, and she sensed in her body that she was cured of her illness.

Blind man of Bethsaida

[17]They come to Bethsaida, and they bring him a blind man, and plead with him to touch him. [18]He took the blind man by the hand and led him out of the village. And he spat into his eyes, and placed his hands on him, and started questioning him, "Do you see anything?"

[19]And he looked up and began to say, "I see human figures, as though they were trees walking around." [20]Then he put his hands on his eyes a second time. And he opened his eyes, and his sight was restored, and he saw everything clearly.

Blind Bartimaeus

[21]Then they come to Jericho. As he was leaving Jericho with his disciples and a good-sized crowd, Bartimaeus, a blind beggar, the son of Timaeus, was sitting by the wayside. [22]When he heard that it was Jesus the Nazarene, he began to shout, "Son of David, Jesus, have mercy on me!"

²³And many kept yelling at him to shut up, but he shouted all the louder, "Son of David, have mercy on me!"

²⁴Jesus paused and said, "Call him over here!"

They called to the blind man, "Be brave, get up, he's calling you!" ²⁵So he threw off his cloak, and jumped to his feet, and went over to Jesus.

²⁶In response Jesus said, "What do you want me to do for you?"

The blind man said to him, "Rabbi, I want to see again."

²⁷And Jesus said to him, "Get going; your trust has cured you." And right away he regained his sight, and he started following him on the way.

Invaluable advice

The itinerant teacher

And from there he gets up and goes to the territory of Judea and across the Jordan, and again crowds gather around him. And again, as usual, he started teaching them.

17:1
MARK 10:1
Source: Mark

Give to beggars

²Give to those who beg from you; and don't turn away those who want to borrow from you.

17:2
MATT 5:42
Luke 6:30
Source: Q

Lend without return

³If you have money, don't lend it at interest. ⁴Instead, give [it] to someone from whom you won't get it back. ⁵If you lend to those from whom you hope to gain, what merit is there in that? Even sinners lend to sinners, in order to get as much in return.

17:3–5
THOM 95:1–2
LUKE 6:34
Matt 5:42
Sources: Thomas, Q

17:6–7
MARK 10:23, 25
Matt 19:23–24
Luke 18:24–25
GNaz 6:5b
Source: Mark

Eye of the needle

⁶How difficult it is for those with money to enter God's empire! ⁷It's easier for a camel to squeeze through the eye of a needle than for the wealthy to get into the empire of God!

Two masters

17:8–9
LUKE 16:13
Matt 6:24
Thom 47:2
Sources: Q,
Thomas

[8]No servant can be a slave to two masters. That slave will either hate one and love the other, or be devoted to one and disdain the other. [9]You can't be enslaved to both God and mammon.

Rich farmer

17:10–12
THOM 63:1–4
Luke 12:16–20
Sources: Thomas,
Luke

[10]There was a rich man who had a great deal of money. [11]He said, "I shall invest my money so that I may sow, reap, plant, and fill my storehouses with produce, that I may lack nothing." [12]These were the things he was thinking in his heart, but that very night he died.

Saving one's life

17:13
LUKE 17:33
Matt 10:39; 16:25
Luke 9:24
John 12:25
Mark 8:35
Sources: Q, John,
Mark

[13]Whoever tries to hang on to life will lose it, but whoever loses it will preserve it.

Castrated for the empire

17:14
MATT 19:12
Source: Matthew

[14]There are castrated men who were born that way, and there are castrated men who were castrated by others, and there are castrated men who castrated themselves because of the empire of Heaven. If you can accept this <teaching>, do so.

Hospitality

Friend at midnight

Suppose you have a friend who comes to you in the middle of the night and says to you, "Friend, lend me three loaves, ²for a friend of mine on a trip has just shown up and I have nothing to offer him." ³And suppose you reply, "Stop bothering me. The door is already locked and my children and I are in bed. I can't get up to give you anything."

⁴I'm telling you, even though you won't get up and give him anything out of friendship, you will get up and give him whatever he needs because of his shameless behavior.

18:1–4
LUKE 11:5–8
Source: Luke

18:5–7
MATT 7:9–11
Luke 11:11–13
Source: Q

Good gifts

⁵Who among you would hand a son a stone when he's asking for bread? ⁶Again, who would hand him a snake when he's asking for fish? Of course no one would! ⁷So if you, worthless as you are, know how to give your children good gifts, isn't it much more likely that your Father in the heavens will give good things to those who ask him?

Shrewd advice

Mountain city

A city sitting on top of a mountain can't be concealed.

19:1
MATT 5:14
Thomas 32
Sources: Matthew, Thomas

Lamp and bushel

2Nor do people light a lamp and put it under a bushel basket, but instead on a lampstand, where it sheds light for everyone in the house.

19:2
MATT 5:15
Mark 4:21
Luke 8:16; 11:33
Thom 33:2–3
Sources: Mark, Thomas

By their fruit

3You'll know who they are by what they produce. Since when do people pick grapes from thorns or figs from thistles?

19:3
MATT 7:16
Luke 6:43–44
Thom 45:1
Sources: Q, Thomas

Fig tree without figs

4A man had a fig tree growing in his vineyard; he came looking for fruit on it but didn't find any.

5So he said to the vinekeeper, "See here, for three years in a row I've come looking for fruit on this tree, and haven't found any. Cut it down. Why should it suck the nutrients out of the soil?"

6In response he says to him, "Let it stand, sir, one more year, until I get a chance to dig around it and work in some manure. 7Maybe it will produce next year; but if it doesn't, we can go ahead and cut it down."

19:4–7
LUKE 13:6–9
Source: Luke

Insipid salt

19:8
LUKE 14:34
MARK 9:50
Matt 5:13
Sources: Mark, Q

[8] Salt is good, but if it loses its zing, how will it be renewed?

In Jerusalem

Temple incident

They come to Jerusalem. And he went into the temple and began throwing the vendors and the customers out of the temple area, and he knocked over the currency exchange tables, along with the chairs of the dove merchants. ²Then he started teaching and saying to them, "Don't the scriptures say, 'My house shall be designated a house of prayer for all peoples'? But you have turned it into 'a hideout for bandits'!"

Emperor and God

³They showed Jesus a gold coin and said to him, "Caesar's people demand taxes from us."

⁴He said to them, "Give Caesar what belongs to Caesar, give God what belongs to God."

Paralytic by the pool

⁵In Jerusalem, by the Sheep <Gate>, there is a pool, called *Bethzatha* in Hebrew. It has five colonnades, ⁶among which numerous invalids—blind, lame, paralyzed—were usually lying around. ⁷One man had been crippled for thirty-eight years. ⁸Jesus observed him lying there and realized he had been there a long time.

20:1-2
MARK 11:15, 17
Matt 21:12–13;
19:45–46
John 2:14–15
Sources: Mark,
John

20:3-4
THOM 100:1–3
Mark 12:13–17
Matt 22:15–22
Luke 20:21
EgerG 3:1–6
Sources: Mark,
Thomas, Egerton
Gospel

20:5-11
JOHN 5:2–3, 5–9
Source: John

"Do you want to get well?" he asks him.

⁹The crippled man replied, "Sir, I don't have anyone to put me in the pool when the water is agitated; while I'm trying to get in someone else beats me to it."

¹⁰"Get up, pick up your mat, and walk around," Jesus tells him.

¹¹And at once the man recovered; he picked up his mat and started walking.

The passion

The arrest

An armed force showed up at the place where Jesus and his followers were gathered. ²Because Jesus had often gone to that place, the one who was about to turn him in knew the place too. ³And they laid hands on him and seized him. ⁴And all his followers deserted him and ran away.

21:1
MARK 14:43
Matt 26:47
Luke 22:47
Source: Mark

21:2
JOHN 18:1–2
Source: John

Before the high priest

⁵And they brought Jesus before the chief priest.

21:3
MARK 14:46
Matt 26:50
Luke 22:54
John 18:12
Sources: Mark, John

Before Pilate

⁶The chief priests bound Jesus and led him away and turned him over to Pilate.

⁷Pilate had Jesus flogged, and turned him over to be crucified.

21:4
MARK 14:50
Matt 26:56
Source: Mark

The crucifixion

⁸And they bring him to the place Golgotha (which means "Place of the Skull"). ⁹And they crucify him, and they divide up his clothes, casting lots to see who would get what.

¹⁰Now some women were observing from a distance, among whom were Mary of Magdala, and Mary the mother of James the younger and Joses,

21:5
MARK 14:53
Matt 26:57
Luke 22:54
John 18:13
Sources: Mark, John

21:6–7
MARK 15:1, 15
Matt 27:1–2, 26
cont.→

Luke 23:1
John 18:28; 19:1, 16
Sources: Mark,
John

21:8–9
MARK 15:22, 24
Matt 27:33, 35
Luke 23:33
John 19:17–18
Sources: Mark,
John

21:10–11
MARK 15:40–41
Matt 27:55–56
Luke 23:49
John 19:25
Sources: Mark,
John

21:12
MARK 15:37
Matt 27:50
Luke 23:46
John 19:30
Sources: Mark,
John

and Salome. [11]These women had regularly followed and assisted him when he was in Galilee, along with many other women who had come up to Jerusalem in his company.

The death

[12]Then Jesus breathed his last.

Epilogue

Pillars & pioneers

Appearance to Mary of Magdala

Jesus appeared first to Mary of Magdala, from whom he had driven out seven demons. ²She went and told those who were close to him, who were mourning and weeping. ³But when those folks heard that he was alive and had been seen by her, they did not believe it.

vv. 1–3
PSMARK 16:9–11
Matt 28:9–10
John 20:1–2, 11–18
Sources: Pseudo-Mark, Matthew, John

Mary's vision

⁴Mary of Magdala said, "I saw the Master in a vision."

Appearance to Peter

⁵ He was seen by Cephas (Peter).

v. 4
MARY 7:1
MATT 28:9–10
JOHN 20:11–18
PSMARK 16:9–11
Sources: Gospel of Mary, Matthew, John, Pseudo-Mark

Appearance to Paul

⁶Last of all, as to one in whose birth God's purpose seemed to have miscarried, he was seen by me as well.

v. 5
1 COR 15:5
LUKE 24:34
Sources: Paul, Luke

Pillars of the Jerusalem community

⁷James, the lord's brother, and Cephas (Peter), and John, the son of Zebedee, were the reputed pillars of the Jerusalem community.

v. 6
1 COR 15:8
Cf. Acts 9:3–19;
22:1–16; 26:9–18
Sources: Paul, Luke

Gospel for the Jews and Gentiles

⁸They recognized that God had entrusted me with the task of announcing God's world-transforming message to the uncircumcised, just as Peter had been entrusted with taking it to the circumcised.

v. 7
GAL 2:9
Source: Paul

v. 8
GAL 2:7
Source: Paul

Notes

Birth, childhood, & family of Jesus

Prol 1

MATT 1:1; LUKE 3:34

In popular piety, all Judeans were descendants of Abraham, the father of the race. There is no reason to believe that records existed to verify the actual ancestors of Jesus. The genealogies of Jesus are therefore fictions that attempt to provide Jesus with illustrious royal ancestors and his followers with honor.

Prol 2

MATT 1:16; LUKE 1:27

Outside the birth and childhood stories in Matthew (chaps. 1–2) and Luke (chaps. 1–2, 3:23–38), Mary is mentioned in the New Testament only in Mark 6:3, in the parallel Matt 13:55, and Acts 1:14. Joseph is mentioned as Jesus' father only in Luke 4:22, John 1:45, and 6:42, again outside the birth and childhood stories of Matthew and Luke.

Prol 3

MATT 2:1; LUKE 1:5

Herod the Great died in 4 BCE.

Prol 4

LUKE 2:21; MATT 1:25

Jesus was probably circumcised in accordance with Jewish practice. Jesus is his Greek name, Yeshua his Aramaic name. The name may be the most reliable piece of information we have about the sage from Nazareth. We have no other reliable information about Jesus' childhood. Legends that Jesus visited India and Tibet during his youth are all late and without historical foundation.

Prol 5
MARK 6:3

Jesus may have adopted the vocation of Joseph, who was a woodworker or artisan. In Mark 6:3, Jesus is referred to as a *tekton*, often translated as carpenter. Matthew (13:55) changes this to *tekton's* son. A woodworker was an artisan, probably itinerant, which placed Jesus or Jesus' father at the bottom of the economic ladder. More generally, Jesus belonged to the peasant class and may have engaged in farming since his parables draw frequently on images from agriculture.

Prol 6
MARK 6:3

That Jesus was known as Mary's son suggests some aberration in his birth. The customary way to identify a son was in relation to the father.

Prol 7
MARK 6:3

Jesus' family included three or four brothers as well as unnamed sisters. Matthew (13:55) adds the name of Joseph or Joses as the fourth brother. According to Paul (1 Cor 9:5), the brothers of Jesus were married.

Prol 8–9
JOHN 1:45–46

Jesus is often identified by his hometown Nazareth. He is never identified by Bethlehem, his alleged birthplace. This suggests that Jesus was actually born in Nazareth, contrary to the claim of the legendary birth stories.

Prol 10–12

MARK 3:21; MATT 13:57

Jesus' brothers and sisters were apparently not in sympathy with his cause during his lifetime.

Prol 13–14

GAL 1:9; 2:9

According to Paul, Jesus' brother James later became a leader in the Jerusalem congregation. He was known as a "pillar" along with Simon Peter (Cephas) and John.

Prol 15

1 COR 15:7

According to Paul, James claimed a revelatory vision or experience of Jesus after Jesus' death. James was probably martyred in 62 CE in Jerusalem (Josephus, *Antiquities of the Jews* 20.9.1; Eusebuis, *Ecclesiastical History* 2.23.1–18, quoting Hegesippus). The family of Jesus later may have played a central role in the leadership of the early Jerusalem community (Eusebius, *Ecclesiastical History* 3.11.1; 3.19.1–20.7, again quoting Hegesippus) although the dynastic possibilities were evidently not followed.

John the Baptizer & Jesus

1:1–3

MARK 1:4–6

The claim that John wore a camel hair mantel and had a leather belt about his waist recalls the description of Elijah in 2 Kings 1:8 and corresponds to the depiction of a prophet's attire in Zech 13:4. For that reason, the Fellows were skeptical about this piece of information and colored it gray.

1:4

MATT 3:1–2

This statement probably accurately summarizes the preaching of John. However, Mark ascribes the same message to Jesus (1:15). See the note on 2:1 for the reasons the Fellows think the ascription here is correct.

1:5–14

LUKE 3:7–15

Much of the discourse attributed to John was colored gray by the Fellows, since although these words probably reflected John's preaching, they would not have been remembered in detail. The Fellows were aware of the competition between the followers of John and those of Jesus that continued long after the deaths of both men. Gray was therefore the correct choice.

1:15–16

MARK 1:7–8

John the Baptizer did anticipate the arrival of a messiah who would succeed him, but it is doubtful that he compared his own water baptism with a future spirit baptism. That sounds like a Christian touch. The Fellows colored v. 16 gray.

1:21–31

MATT 4:1–11

The Fellows of the Jesus Seminar voted the core of the temptation story gray rather than black on the grounds that Jesus may have undergone some sort of vision quest in the desert. However, they regarded the specific content of this story as a fiction. The devil and Satan are of course mythic figures. Although fictive, the story contains some interesting points. Jesus is represented as rejecting the miraculous approach to messiahship and as refusing to supply bread to the hungry as the means of winning approval. The

Lukan version of the ordeal story was cast in terms of competing wonder workers, while Matthew's version pits one scholar against another. Both the gospels of Matthew and Luke, in following the Q Gospel, depict the ordeal of Jesus at the outset of his public ministry. The temptation story is thus a kind of anticipatory counterweight to the later stories of the feeding of the multitudes and the nature wonders.

Jesus announces God's empire

2:1–2

MARK 1:14

According to Mark 1:15, Jesus proclaims that God's empire is at hand, he calls on people to undergo a change of heart, and he invites them to put their trust in the good news. The Fellows voted this summary black as being the work of Mark, who borrowed the content from the preaching of John the Baptizer. It is more accurate to present the authentic beatitudes as a summary of the gospel of Jesus than to have Jesus echo the message of John. The Fellows did conclude that Jesus had been a follower of the Baptizer. Whether Jesus began his career before or after the imprisonment and death of John was unsettled. The Jesus Seminar became convinced that Jesus was not an apocalyptic prophet like John, because many of his parables and many of his aphorisms do not portray him as anticipating imminent divine judgment. This opening frame is only that. None of the brief settings of the *Gospel of Jesus* reflects an actual event. In fact, many of the sayings may well have been uttered at meals Jesus shared.

The term "empire" (*basileia* in Greek) refers primarily to the notion of "effective presence or rule," and not to a particular location. It was the equivalent of the Latin *imperium*. For example, the emperor's imperium or effective presence was felt in Israel through the occupation forces. Later gospel writers such as Matthew begin to associate the "empire" with "heaven" (where the God of Israel is sovereign).

2:6–8
MARK 10:13–15

Jesus probably made some pronouncement about children and God's empire to correspond to his congratulations to the poor, hungry, and sad. Whether the original disciples opposed his openness to children is uncertain; such opposition may reflect resistance in the later Markan community.

2:23–26
THOM 97:1–4

For a positive version of this astonishing parable see GJ 15:4–7 (Thom 113:1–4).

2:40
LUKE 12:34

While this saying was voted gray by the Fellows, it reflects very much the intense sense of purpose and shrewd peasant wisdom found in the authentic sayings.

In the company of Jesus

3:1–5
MARK 1:16–20

The Fellows agreed by a substantial majority that Jesus had been a disciple of John the Baptizer and that some followers of John subsequently became disciples of Jesus. It therefore seems likely that Jesus first met some of his key followers during his connection with the Baptizer in the Jordan valley.

The stories in 3:1-6 follow the usual format of a call story, wherein a teacher calls on a follower to make a life-changing decision to leave behind known social ties and conventions and to enter a company centered around a new vision of life. The stereotypical character of the call stories in Mark 1:16–20 prompted the Fellows to color these accounts gray.

Luke substitutes the anecdote about the miraculous catch of fish (5:1–11) for Mark's twin stories. The Fellows were clear that Luke's account was a Lukan invention. It was therefore designated black.

The twin stories in the Gospel of John (1:35–42, 43–51) were also colored black as fictions, even though the Fellows agreed that Jesus probably recruited his first disciples from among followers of John. Elements in the Johannine version clearly reflect later perspectives of that community (for example, John recognizes Jesus as "the lamb of God," and Philip tells Nathanael that "We've found the one Moses wrote about in the Law, and the prophets mention too"). John's version may be correct in indicating that Jesus first recruited disciples from among John's followers while they were all still working in the Jordan valley.

3:8–10
LUKE 8:1–3
This is a Lukan construction, summarizing Jesus' activity in Galilee as an itinerant sage and healer. The Fellows were convinced that women were part of the company of Jesus. But the description of Mary of Magdala's healing as well as the (unverifiable) mentioning of Joanna and Susanna may reflect the later concerns of the Lukan community.

3:11–12
LUKE 9:57–58
The saying is authentically Jesus; the setting may be contrived.

3:13–14

LUKE 9:59–60

Once again the saying is authentically Jesus, but the setting may be fictitious.

3:15

MATT 5:39

The usual translation "Do not resist evil" does not convey the sense of the Greek. Literally the verse says: "Do not stand over against on the same level someone who intends harm." This is not advice to do nothing; rather it urges response on a different level. It goes beyond the alternatives of fight or flight. This advice was taken to heart by Mahatma Gandhi and then, in turn, by Martin Luther King, Jr.

3:16

MATT 5:40

Peasants usually had only two articles of clothing: a shirt and a coat.

3:17

MATT 5:41

A Roman soldier could only command someone to carry his 50 pound pack for one Roman mile. To extend this could entail punishment for the offending soldier.

3:19

THOM 42

Thomas 42 is usually translated as "Be passersby!" but this does not fully convey the probable Greek version of the Coptic. This shortest saying attributed to Jesus may well reflect his challenge to others to "Get going," "Get up," "Be on the way!" It points out the itinerant nature of Jesus' companions. The scholars of the Seminar were divided on this saying, with some greatly in favor and others opposed. The decision was usually based on how each translated the Coptic saying.

Upsetting expectations

4:1–2

MARK 1:21–22

Mark created these verses as a narrative transition. Because they reflect the typical exaggeration of a later community, the Fellows designed them as gray. Yet Jesus did appear to teach with a distinctive voice, using aphorisms, parables and stories. Jesus is described as speaking often in local synagogues.

4:4–20

MATT 20:1–15

The Roman denarius was the usual wage for a day's labor.

4:23–37

MATT 25:14–28

A talent was a unit of weight of approximately 75 lbs. It would be the equivalent of 20 years work for a peasant laborer.

Powers at work

5:1–5

MARK 1:35–39

The Fellows decided that it was highly probable that Jesus practiced prayer in seclusion, that he preached in the synagogues of Galilee, and that he drove out what were thought to be demons. Although colored black in *The Acts of Jesus* as a fiction, this story is included here because it depicts typical activities of the historical Jesus. In other words, the story is what may be called a "true fiction."

The ancients would speak of situations beyond their control by using mythic speech. Illness was understood as an invasion by an outside force or power.

The performance and language of exorcism was a dramatic response to a grave situation.

5:6–11
MARK 1:23–28

This is a standard account of an exorcism: the demon recognizes the exorcist; the exorcist orders the demon to depart with a command; the demon obeys under protest; there is some indication that the exorcism worked; bystanders verify the healing.

The Fellows were dubious that the story as Mark (and Luke 4:33–37) reports it is a description of a specific event. They therefore colored it gray, as they did all the other accounts of exorcism. Nevertheless, the Seminar concluded that Jesus did practice exorcism and that this story reflects that practice.

All illness was seen as an invasion by forces beyond the sick person's control. Thus, every healing could be understood as an exorcism.

5:17
LUKE 11:20

Matthew's version (12:28) reads: "But if I drive out demons with the spirit of God, then the empire of God has come for you."

5:22–29
MARK 7:24–30

The Fellows were relatively certain that this anecdote contains a kernel of historical truth. Yet they could not agree on precisely which elements were historical and which fictions. They were agreed, however, that Jesus and the woman had an exchange of witticisms in which the woman got the better of Jesus. They concluded that it was unlikely the disciples would have invented such a story for their hero. The response given by Jesus could reflect the prejudice of the period against non-Jews or an attempt by Jesus to use such prejudice to get an unexpected rejoinder. Since it is impossible to edit out the fictional parts of the anecdote, the entire story was included in *The Gospel of Jesus.*

5:30–32
LUKE 11:24–26

It was usually assumed that exorcised demons did not return to their previous human hosts. Yet this saying suggests that demons, once deprived of a human home, were thought to wander through "waterless places" seeking a new abode. (Demons were thought to inhabit "wet places," such as outhouses and springs and human bodies.) When they are unable to relocate, it was thought that they would eventually return to their previous habitation, bring additional vile spirits with them, thereby making the second condition of the possessed worse than at first.

Death of John the Baptizer

6:1–12
MARK 6:14–29

The story of the beheading of John the Baptizer probably reflects historical fact. Details of the story are undoubtedly the product of the storyteller's imagination, but the basic elements may well be accurate. John the Baptizer probably did criticize Herod Antipas for his wife-swapping proclivities, and Herodias, Herod's new wife, may have held a grudge against John as a consequence. The role Salome, Herodias' daughter, played in the story is probably fictive, but the beheading of John is not. He was probably executed at Herod's wilderness palace at Machaerus. Other details of the story recorded by Mark are too far-fetched to be treated as historical. Luke omits the account of John's beheading.

Surprising vision & advice

7:1

MARK 2:13

This is one of Mark's narrative connectives. In it Mark depicts Jesus as frequenting the Sea of Galilee, where he was often surrounded by crowds. Naturally, the teacher could do nothing other than teach. These typifications the Fellows regarded as essentially accurate.

7:3–5

LUKE 6:27, 32–33

Matthew's version (5:44, 46–47) varies slightly from Luke:

> [44]Love your enemies. [46]Tell me, if you love those who love you, why should you be rewarded for that? Even the toll collectors do as much, don't they? [47]And if you greet only your friends, what have you done that is exceptional? Even the pagans do as much, don't they?

7:28–36

JOHN 8:3–11

The Fellows gave the story of the woman accused of adultery a gray rating. Yet, because it represents Jesus associating with sinners and as an advocate of mercy, the Fellows thought it might reflect the disposition of the historical Jesus. It is what might be called a true fiction. In any case, it is a fragment of a lost gospel that somehow got attached to either the Gospel of John or the Gospel of Luke in some early manuscripts.

A place at the table

8:1–5

MARK 2:15–17

We have omitted certain phrases from the fictive narrative frame. It is often overlooked that the sayings of

Jesus may have first been uttered as part of the conversation at meals.

8:6–7
LUKE 15:1–2

Luke has created this transitional connective; it has no parallels in Mark or Matthew. Yet it appears to be typical of Jesus' public life, as indicated by other anecdotes in the gospels. The Fellows gave it a gray designation but took it to be representative of Jesus' activity and the response to it.

8:8–10
LUKE 10:5, 7–8

The peace greeting, "shalom," was a standard greeting on entering someone's house. Because it doesn't tell anything specific about Jesus, the Fellows designated this verse (v. 8) gray. However, the advice to eat and drink whatever is offered does go beyond the purity regulations.

8:11–12
MARK 2:18–19

The evangelist or some storyteller before him makes additions in Mark 2:20-21:

> [20]But the days will come when the groom is taken away from them, and then they will fast on that day. [21]Nobody sews a piece of unshrunk cloth on an old garment, otherwise the new, unshrunk patch pulls away from the old and creates a worse tear.

The addition indicates how the later Jesus community restored fasting among its practices without contradicting its memory of the historical Jesus, who did not fast. The addition also demonstrates how the later gospel writers regarded their developing traditions as superior to the earlier.

8:13–14

THOM 47:3–4

In this saying, the old is still superior to the new. However, as the Jesus traditions developed, the tendency was to reverse the relationship: the new emerging Jesus group became superior to its Jewish matrix. Luke even quotes the common proverb, "Aged wine is just fine" (Luke 5:39b). The Fellows judged the version in Thomas and Luke (5:37–39) to be an earlier version and therefore something the historical Jesus might have said.

Jesus & purity matters

9:1–5

MARK 7:1–5

The criticism is here directed against Jesus' disciples (v. 2), which suggests that the report may have been assimilated to the situation in Galilee after the death of Jesus, perhaps even after the destruction of the temple in 70 CE. Nevertheless, it seems likely that Jesus failed to observe all the purity codes and so may have drawn criticism for not washing his hands in the traditional fashion prior to eating. This facet of his behavior comports with his refusal to observe kosher and his willingness to eat with persons considered unclean.

9:6–8

MARK 7:14–16

The saying in v. 8 is probably a cliché that Jesus may or may not have employed. It has been added now and again after sayings, especially those difficult to understand. It served as a wise directional for the listener. Because it is probably something many teachers said to their pupils, the Fellows colored it gray.

Celebration

10:1-5

LUKE 7:31-53

The Fellows were divided in their interpretation of this complex. Some thought that the reference in v. 4 to "the Human One" precluded the possibility that the complex stemmed from Jesus. Others held that the phrase was Jesus' way of referring to himself in the third person. A divided vote yielded a gray average. Yet all the Fellows agreed that the characterizations fit what we otherwise know of Jesus and John the Baptizer. The final verse reflects a prevailing Jewish Wisdom tradition that Lady Wisdom (*Sophia/ Hokmah*) not only manifested herself throughout time but had offspring. Both John the Baptizer and Jesus would have been thought of as "sons of Lady Wisdom" in this tradition.

10:6-7

LUKE 15:8-9

The Greek drachma was the equivalent of one day's wage.

10:11-12

MATT 13:44

The version in Thomas (109) has developed along different lines. In the Thomas version, the person who discovers the treasure becomes a moneylender which in Thomas (95) is a forbidden occupation:

> The Father's empire is like a man who had a treasure hidden in his field but didn't know it. ²And when he died he left it to his son. The son did not know about it either. He took over the field and sold it. ³The buyer went plowing, discovered the treasure, and began to lend money at interest to whomever he wished.

10:13-14

THOM 76:1-2

Matthew's alternate version (13:45-46) reads:

> [45]Again, the empire of Heaven is like some merchant looking for beautiful pearls. [46]When he finds one priceless pearl, he sells everything he owns and buys it.

Sabbath observance

11:5-11

MARK 3:1-5

The Fellows of the Jesus Seminar, in concert with many other scholars, concluded that this story is largely fictive. However, because they think it may contain the kernel of a historical event, they colored it gray. The Fellows believe that Jesus questioned sabbath regulations on at least one occasion (pink), and this story along with Luke 14:1-6 was the basis of that decision. Thus, while the story does not depict an actual event and may reflect later synagogal debates, it still could indicate the kind of liberties Jesus took with sabbath restrictions.

Kinship in the empire

12:1-3

MARK 3:20-21

Both Matthew and Luke chose to suppress the tradition that Jesus' family thought him demon-possessed—mad. However, the rumor is also reported in the Gospel of John (10:19-21), and it is unlikely that the storytellers of the developing Jesus movement would have invented the charge.

12:4

JOHN 10:20

The charge, that many people thought Jesus mad, is less certain than that his family believed him to be out of his mind—the latter surely would not have been invented by the later Jesus community. The Fellows colored the statement in the Gospel of John gray. It is included here because it lends credence to the Markan story.

12:5-9
MARK 3:31-35
The Thomas version (99) reads:

> The disciples said to him, "Your brothers and your mother are standing outside."
> [2]He said to them, "Those here who do what my Father wants are my brothers and my mother. [3]They are the ones who will enter my Father's empire."

12:10-11
LUKE 14:25-26
The narrative setting in v. 10 is probably a fiction of the evangelist.

12:12-19
MARK 6:1-6
The narrative connective in v. 12 is a fiction of Mark, yet the incident probably did take place in his hometown.

In parables

13:1-3
MARK 4:1-2
The author of the Gospel of Mark depicts Jesus teaching a crowd from a boat on the Sea of Galilee. These are typifications and are not intended to represent a single event. Mark affixes the collection of parables (Mark 4:3-34) to this introduction (Mark 4:1-2). We have followed his example, except that the collection of parables employed in *The Gospel of Jesus* is rather different than the one Mark put together.

13:30

THOM 65:1–7

A lacuna in the Thomas text makes the Coptic here uncertain; the hole can be filled in to read either "good man" or "greedy man."

13:37–39

THOM 98:1–3

The Fellows took three votes on this parable. The Seminar moved from a vote registering this saying as historically unlikely (gray) to seeing this provocative parable as quite possibly (pink) from the historical Jesus. The decision for authenticity came upon noting that this saying is not an endorsement for violence but a likening of the Father's empire to the action of an intelligent agent. The objection that the historical Jesus could not use violent language was found to be a modern projection and an oversight of the linguistic repertoires of first-century Israel. Some Fellows also saw in this saying a significant difference from two similar sayings that were voted as not from the historical Jesus (the tower builder, Luke 14:28–30, and the warring king, Luke 14:31–32). The proverbial wisdom of the Lukan sayings was turned upside down by the act of a peasant against an oppressive bully.

Public & private piety

14:1

MATT 6:6

The weighted average fell into the gray category, although 58% of the Fellows voted red or pink. The debate centered on whether Jesus had anything to say about prayer. Prayer in the ancient world was spoken aloud in a public venue. To be advised to pray (still speaking) in a closet would have been seen as comic and somewhat subversive.

14:2–4

LUKE 11:2

Jesus' mode of addressing God should be compared with a regulation found in the Manual of Discipline, one of the Dead Sea Scrolls. The Manual contains a charter for the Essene communities, including the one at Qumran. Among the regulations is this (col. 6:27–7:2):

> Anyone who speaks aloud the Most Holy Name of God, whether as a curse or simply blurts it out when under duress, or for any other reason, or while he is reading a book or praying, is to be expelled, never to be readmitted to the community.

In contrast, Jesus playfully combines an informal, even familiar address ("Abba"/"Dad"—which other Jews of that time also warmly expressed), with the admonition to revere the Holy Name, viz. Yahweh, which he apparently never employs. There is a hint of humor in this combination.

Signs of God's empire

15:1–3

MARK 8:11–13

It is very probable that people in Jesus' day expected prophets to be able to provide some special omen to demonstrate that they had been authorized by God to say and do what they were saying and doing. Jesus is believed to have refused such requests, as this anecdote indicates.

15:8–10

LUKE 17:20–21

This saying and the preceding one are probably derived from the same original—if there was a single prototype. Both of these sayings would have challenged listeners to detect God's empire as effectively present, not postponed in some future hope. Both undermine an apocalyptic timetable.

Six healings

16:1–2

MATT 8:14–15

Matthew's is a simpler version of the anecdote in Mark (1:29–31).

16:3–5

MARK 1:40–42

The Egerton Gospel version (EgerG 2:1-3) is derived from oral tradition, and, because it does not reproduce any of the idiosyncrasies found in Mark, it represents an independent source. It has some interesting variations on the story:

> Just then a leper comes up to him and says, "Teacher, Jesus, in wandering around with lepers and eating with them in the inn, I became a leper myself. [2]If you want to, I'll be made clean." [3]The master said to him, "Okay—you're clean!" And at once his leprosy disappeared from him.

16:6–12

MARK 2:1–5a, 11–12

Although they designated parts of this story gray, the Fellows were relatively certain that Jesus told a lame man to pick up his mat; they were also confident that Jesus healed a lame man. Readers will notice that there is often a change of tense in some passages (e.g., from past to present). This change in tense reflects the Greek of the original, indicating the vivid speech of oral performance. The Gospel of Mark often illustrates this.

16:13–16

MARK 5:24–25, 27, 29

As printed here, this story has been edited down to
its core, which may well reflect an actual event in the
career of the historical Jesus. Either the evangelist or
storytellers prior to him elaborated the story by providing fictive details to make it more impressive.

16:17–20

MARK 8:22–25

As an ancient healer (or shaman) Jesus would have
been exorcising the powers that had overwhelmed a
victim. Such actions would not make Jesus unique at
that time. But these healings, coupled with the words
of Jesus, would have indicated to witnesses that the
God of Israel was effectively present. While today
such healings are explained as psychosomatic ther-
apy, the ancient audience would have recognized such
healings as demonstrations of real power. According
to the Gospel of John, Peter and Andrew were from
Bethsaida, a fishing village on the northern shore of
the Sea of Galilee (1:44). Jesus is also reported to have
cured the man born blind (John 9:1–7).

16:21–27

MARK 10:46–52

According to the sequence of events in Mark, Jesus
now recrosses the Jordan at Jericho on his way up to
Jerusalem (10:46). He there encounters a blind beggar
who addresses him as "Son of David," implying that
he was the counterpart of Solomon who was famous
for his miraculous cures. The correlation of trust
with cure in v. 27 (Mark 10:52) is a Markan motif that
appears elsewhere in his stories of cures. The note
that the blind beggar, now with his sight restored,
became a follower of Jesus is probably also a Markan

touch. The core of the story, which reports the cure of a blind man, may well be historical. It is comparable to the account of the blind man of Bethsaida, 16:17–20, above. In both cases Jesus was performing as a shaman.

A similar story is found in John 9:1, 6–7, the man born blind:

> As Jesus was leaving he saw a man who had been blind from birth. ⁶With that he spat on the ground, made mud with his saliva, and smeared the mud on the man's eyes. ⁷Then Jesus said to him, "Go, rinse off in the pool of Siloam" (the name means "Emissary"). So he went over, rinsed off <his eyes>, and came back with his sight restored.

It is possible that this story in the Gospel of John and the report of the blind man of Bethsaida (16:17–20) may have evolved from the same basic incident. The cure is effected with spittle in both cases. Or, the Johannine report may have been developed out of the account of Blind Bartimaeus. It is impossible to reconstruct the history of these reports with confidence. Yet it seems likely that the cure of at least one blind person circulated in the oral traditions about Jesus at an early time. The propensity of the gospel writers to alter and elaborate reports at will does not breed confidence in the specific details of any of the versions.

Invaluable advice

17:1

MARK 10:1

At some point in his public career, Jesus decided to go south to Judea and Jerusalem. His way south may have prompted him to cross the Jordan close to the Sea of Galilee, walk south in Transjordan, and then recross the Jordan at Jericho. By using this route he would have avoided contact with Samaritans who were sometimes hostile to pilgrims on their way to Jerusalem. The geography of Mark is somewhat garbled: he says that Jesus crossed the Jordan into the territory of Judea, which did not extend east of the Jordan. Nevertheless, the general movement of Jesus southward is probably historical. As an itinerant, Jesus undoubtedly taught as he walked along. Locating Jesus' departure for Jerusalem at this point in the story is purely arbitrary both in Mark and in *The Gospel of Jesus.*

17:6–7
MARK 10:23, 25
There have been numerous attempts to avoid the comic note of this aphorism. Assuming that the historical Jesus could not be humorous, some readers have tried to explain the joke away. Some have claimed that the "eye of a needle" was actually the name of a gate in Jerusalem but there is no evidence for this. The attempt to reduce the word "camel" to "rope" in Aramaic in order to render the saying "reasonable" fails to see that an oral performer in the ancient world would play with images that were startling, provocative and memorable. In fact, the interplay of the enormous with the small can be found elsewhere in sayings of the historical Jesus. This surprising opening contrasts with an even more outrageous challenge: that wealth is not a guaranteed mark of divine favor. Even the poor, who shared that cultural given, would have been caught off guard.

17:8–9
LUKE 16:13
Mammon is an Aramaic word for wealth.

In Jerusalem

20:1–2

MARK 11:15, 17

For many of the Fellows it was possible that Jesus created an incident in the temple area, although there are
significant issues with its probability. The Temple area
was enormous (its length was the size of three football
fields; its width one football field) so Jesus could not
have cleared the area of hundreds of pilgrims and he
could not have prevented the merchants from plying
their trade without certain arrest from the Temple
police. The saying of Jesus (GJ 20:2) is actually a
combination of two sayings from Isaiah 56:7 and
Jeremiah 7:11. Such a verbal collage would argue for
a later scribal hand; a major reason for considering
that this scene is fictive. Nevertheless, many fellows
still thought that Jesus precipitated some incident
and that it may have figured in his eventual arrest and
execution.

20:3–4

THOM 100:1–3

The version in the Gospel of Mark (12:13–17) reads:

> [13]And they send some of the Pharisees and the
> Herodians to him to trap him with a riddle. [14]They
> come and say to him, "Teacher, we know that you
> are honest and impartial, because you pay no atten-
> tion to appearances, but instead you teach God's way
> forthrightly. Is it permissible to pay the poll tax to
> Caesar or not? Should we pay or should we not pay?"
>
> [15]But he saw through their trap, and said to them,
> "Why do you provoke me like this? Let me have a
> look at a denarius."
>
> [16]They handed him one, and he says to them,
> "Whose image is this? Whose name is on it?"
>
> They replied, "Caesar's."

¹⁷Jesus said to them, "Pay to Caesar what belongs to Caesar, and to God what belongs to God."

And they were dumbfounded at him.

The Thomas version preserves the core of the original story, which Mark has elaborated into a full-blown narrative segment. In Mark, v. 13 is part of the evangelist's conspiracy theory: Jesus was the victim of a conspiracy against him. The anecdote that develops the riddle and Jesus' clever reply is told in the style of the pronouncement stories so common in hellenistic lore. However, the aphorism reported in both Thomas and Mark probably goes back to Jesus.

20:5–11
JOHN 5:2–3, 5–9
The Fellows colored this story gray because the fourth evangelist has taken an older healing story and revised it to suit the new context he has devised for it. The Johannine story may have been derived ultimately from the same tale that Mark reports in 2:1–12 (16:6–12 above). The note of the pool *Bethzatha* is actually not in Hebrew but in the cognate Aramaic. The name varies considerably among the mss, *Bethesda* being the most widely attested alternative.

The passion

21:2
JOHN 18:1–2
The statements in this and the preceding verse were colored gray by the Fellows. However, a narrative statement to the effect that those who knew Jesus turned him in by taking the temple authorities to the place drew a pink vote. In other words, the Fellows agreed by a slim majority that some of Jesus' followers betrayed the place where the authorities might find him. Jesus himself did not require identification.

21:8

MARK 15:22, 24

The Fellows were convinced that the Romans crucified Jesus. The harshest torture of the empire was reserved for slaves and those who raised their sandal against Rome. This entailed a complete degradation of the victim, who would have been considered polluted and a social outcast. The ultimate effect was to erase the victim from social memory.

Pillars & Pioneers

Epil 1–3

PSMARK 16:9–11

This text is derived from PsMark 16:9–11, which the Seminar colored black. It is used here to express the judgment of the Fellows that Mary of Magdala may have been the first to come to understand the postmortem visions of Jesus in apocalyptic terms of his being raised by the God of Israel, who vindicates the innocent. That conviction is based in part on the account in John 20:1–2, 11–18, which, unfortunately, is linked to the empty tomb story. When the Fellows colored the Johannine version of the appearance to Mary gray, they did so because they could not find Mary's claim expressed elsewhere without ties to the empty tomb. Further, they agreed on two points: Mary was the first to have a vision of the risen Jesus; those to whom Mary reported her experience did not at first believe her. The words of Pseudo-Mark seemed to be the best vehicle to express these two judgments. Of course, the unedited text of Pseudo-Mark does connect Mary's vision with the Easter Sunday morning at the tomb, but in this case it was easily possible to eliminate that connection. On the other hand, the editors saw no way to disentangle the Johannine version of Mary's encounter with the risen Jesus from the setting at the tomb.

Resources

Table of Ancient Gospels

Sayings Gospels
1. The Q Gospel
2. Gospel of Thomas
3. Gospel Oxyrhynchus 1224
4. Secret Book of James
5. Dialogue of the Savior
6. Gospel of Mary

Narrative Gospels
7. Gospel of Mark
8. Gospel of Matthew
9. Gospel of Luke
10. Signs Gospel
11. Gospel of John
12. Gospel of Peter
13. Mystical Gospel of Mark
14. Egerton Gospel
15. Amulet Gospel (Gospel Oxyrhynchus 840)
16. Orphan Gospel Fragment
17. Gospel of the Hebrews
18. Gospel of the Nazoreans
19. Gospel of the Ebionites
20. Gospel of the Savior
21. Gospel of Judas

Infancy Gospels
22. Infancy Gospel of Thomas
23. Infancy Gospel of James

Dates of the Gospels

Stage 1: 50–70 CE
The Q Gospel
First edition of Thomas
Gospel Oxyrhynchus 1224
Signs Gospel
P – First edition of Gospel of Peter

Stage 2: 70–80
Gospel of Mark
Egerton Gospel

Stage 3: 80–90
Gospel of Matthew
Gospel of Thomas

Stage 4: 90–100
Gospel of Luke
Gospel of John

Stage 5: 100–150
Gospel of Peter
Gospel of Mary
Mystical Gospel of Mark
Infancy Gospel of James
Infancy Gospel of Thomas
Secret James
Amulet Gospel (Gospel Oxyrhynchus 840)
Dialogue of the Savior

Stage 6: 150 and beyond
Gospel of the Ebionites
Gospel of the Hebrews
Gospel of the Nazoreans
Gospel of the Savior
Gospel of Judas

Catalogue of Ancient Gospels

The New Testament Gospels

There are four New Testament gospels, as everyone knows. Their order in conventional New Testaments is: Matthew, Mark, Luke, John. Since Mark is the earliest of the four and the probable basis of both Matthew and Luke, in the Scholars Version we have moved Mark to the first position. These gospels, which are narrative gospels (not just collections of Jesus' sayings), provide us with the bulk of basic information we have about Jesus.

Gospel of Mark

An anonymous author composed the Gospel of Mark shortly after the destruction of the Jerusalem temple in 70 CE. Mark may be responsible for forming the first chronological outline of the life of Jesus. A number of scholars argue that Mark constructed the first connected narrative of Jesus' trial and crucifixion, commonly referred to as the passion story. Some others argue that Mark had access to an earlier narrative such as the earliest layer (P) of the Gospel of Peter. The author reflects the Markan community's view that they were the last generation, awaiting the apocalyptic end of time and their vindication at the coming of the Human One.

The Gospel of Mark was attributed to John Mark, a companion of Paul and perhaps an associate of Peter. This attribution, like many others in the ancient world, is the product of pious speculation.

Mark's gospel became the basis for the gospels of Matthew and Luke.

Gospel of Matthew

An anonymous author compiled the Gospel of Matthew sometime after the fall of Jerusalem and before the gathering of the Pharisees at the Council of Jamnia (circa 90 CE). The community of Matthew, either in Galilee or in Western Syria, competed with the Rabbis over the future of Judaism. Both groups were trying to recover from the seismic loss of the temple, the center of Jewish worship. Matthew presents a case for interpreting the Jewish traditions through the prism of the wisdom of God embodied in Jesus. This gospel is dated to about 85 CE.

Matthew was composed in Greek. The author made use of both the Q Gospel and the Gospel of Mark. It is incorrect to say that Matthew was composed in Hebrew by one of the original disciples of Jesus.

Gospel of Luke

Luke-Acts, a two volume work by a single author, places the emergence of the Jesus movement onto the world stage. While many scholars date the Gospel of Luke around the last decade of the first century, recently scholars have dated the Acts of the Apostles to the first quarter of the second century. Together these two documents provide a foundation myth for the origin of the Jesus movement. These volumes display a writer familiar with the style and Greek of the Septuagint. While these volumes may be speaking to mixed communities of Jews and Greeks, the momentum of these texts depicts an ever-successful movement, moving inevitably from Jerusalem to Rome.

The tradition that the author was Luke the physician and companion of Paul goes back to the second

century. However, it is highly improbable that Luke
was a physician and he almost certainly was not a
companion of Paul. As in the case of the other gospels, the author is unknown.

Gospel of John

The Gospel of John was allegedly written by John, son
of Zebedee, one of an inner group of Jesus' companions. According to legend, John lived to a ripe old age
in Ephesus where he composed the gospel, three letters, and possibly the book of Revelation. This legend
is fictive.

The Gospel of John was probably composed to-
ward the close of the first century CE, which makes it
a close contemporary of Matthew and possibly Luke.
It exhibits evidence of having gone through several
editions. Many scholars therefore conclude that John
is the product of a "school," which may indeed have
been formed by the John of the legend.

Its place of origin is unknown. It was clearly created in a hellenistic city of some magnitude with a
strong Jewish community. A city in Asia Minor or
Syria, or possibly Alexandria in Egypt, would do.

Scholars are divided over whether John knew the
synoptic gospels—Mark, Matthew, Luke—so-called
because they take a common view of the life of Jesus,
based as they are on the narrative skeleton of Mark.
The Johannine school may have made use of a "signs"
source, which consisted of a series of healings and
wonders presumably performed by Jesus. The writer
of John may have known of an earlier passion narrative, possibly from an early version of the Gospel of
Peter or from the Gospel of Mark.

In addition to the four New Testament gospels,
there were at least nineteen other gospels, seventeen

of which have survived from antiquity, either in whole or in part. The other two are hypothetical reconstructions.

Sayings Gospels
The Q Gospel
In the view of a great many scholars, Matthew and Luke once knew and used a written collection of the sayings of Jesus in composing their own gospels. If this hypothesis is correct, that source may well have been among the very first gospels reduced to writing. Sayings of the sages were collected throughout the Hellenistic world. The Q Gospel would have been like those other collections of wise sayings in antiquity. Although it did not survive as a separate document, this collection of Jesus' sayings became an important part of Matthew and Luke.

This lost gospel has been dubbed Q from a German word meaning "source" (*Quelle*); it is now usually referred to as the Q Gospel. A reconstructed Q may be found in *The Complete Gospels* and *The Complete Gospel Parallels*.

Gospel of Thomas
The Gospel of Thomas is also a sayings gospel. It contains 114 sayings ascribed to Jesus. It lacks narrative connectives; it does not have a passion story, or appearance stories, or birth and childhood stories. The Coptic text of Thomas was discovered at Nag Hammadi, a place in upper Egypt, in 1945. Three Greek fragments of Thomas had been discovered earlier, but scholars were unable to identify them as fragments of Thomas until the Coptic text was unearthed. There is about a 40% overlap between Q and Thomas.

Gospel Oxyrhynchus 1224
Two tiny fragments of a gospel whose name is unknown were discovered in 1903 at Oxyrhynchus in

Egypt. It contains some very fragmentary sayings of Jesus and has thus been classified as a sayings gospel.

Secret Book of James & Dialogue of the Savior

Two other gospels from Nag Hammadi, Secret James and the Dialogue of the Savior, also provide some data about Jesus, but they have not contributed significantly to the advance of knowledge.

Gospel of Mary

The Gospel of Mary was discovered among papyrus fragments in the Berlin Museum. There are also some scraps of a Greek version of Mary, just as there are Greek scraps of the Gospel of Thomas. Unfortunately, the center portion of Mary is missing. It is still unclear what we will learn from the study of the Gospel of Mary, although Mary is primarily a sayings rather than a narrative gospel.

Other Narrative Gospels

The Signs Gospel

Some scholars believe that a collection of signs that Jesus performed was the precursor of the Gospel of John. Attempts have been made to reconstruct it from the text of John. The Signs Gospel appears to have some stories in common with a similar sequence of miracles in the Gospel of Mark.

The Gospel of Peter

The Gospel of Peter is a fragmentary narrative of the passion and resurrection of Jesus. Some scholars contend that Peter contains the earliest narrative of the arrest, trial and crucifixion of Jesus. The earliest layer may have emerged in Syria sometime before the Jewish War. It has turned out to be part of the fundamental debate about the creation and transmission of the passion narrative.

Mystical Gospel of Mark

Two brief fragments from an early version of the Gospel of Mark were discovered in 1958 and published in 1973. It is called Mystical Gospel of Mark because this version is believed to be intended for only those who had reached a higher stage of initiation. The rest of the Mystical Gospel of Mark has been lost, at least for the present. The two fragments confirm once again that the gospels went through more than one edition in their earlier stages.

Egerton Gospel

The Egerton Gospel is known from a single cluster of fragments that can be dated to the middle of the second century. It preserves a few anecdotes about Jesus that may contain some independent testimony. Egerton is the name of the donor who gave the money to purchase the fragments. Like most other manuscripts of the gospels, Egerton comes from Egypt.

Amulet Gospel (Gospel Oxyrhynchus 840)

This gospel is a very small vellum fragment of a narrative gospel written in a tiny script. It was probably used as an amulet by some Christian folk. Most of the remaining text is devoted to a dispute over purity in the temple precincts. The handwriting suggests that the copy was made in the fourth century CE, although the composition of this gospel probably took place much earlier.

Orphan Gospel Fragment

The story of the woman accused of adultery and brought to Jesus appears in manuscripts of the Gospels of John and Luke. It is what scholars call a floating segment or orphan text. It probably comes from another earlier narrative gospel, the balance of which was lost. The first stone segment survived by being copied into John or Luke.

The Jewish-Christian Gospels

According to some of the scholars of the early church—called Church Fathers—there were three Jewish-Christian gospels: Ebionites, Hebrews, and Nazoreans, by name. The Fathers preserve a few scattered quotations from these gospels. They must be added to our list of sources.

The Gospel of the Savior

Recently, fragments of the Gospel of the Savior were discovered in the Berlin Egyptian Museum by Charles Hedrick and Paul Mirecki. The Gospel of the Savior survives only in Coptic, like the Nag Hammadi Codices. It consists of a dialogue between the savior and the apostles. The author appears to know all four canonical gospels as well as Thomas. The narrative was constructed out of earlier gospel materials.

The fragments are to be dated from the fourth to the seventh centuries CE. They will probably contribute very little new information to the quest for the historical Jesus.

The Gospel of Judas

The Gospel of Judas is a second-century text that knows of earlier gospel traditions. It purports to tell the inside story of the events leading up to the betrayal of Jesus. However, this gospel does not give any new information about the historical Jesus; rather it is concerned primarily with the later developing questions of authority and martyrdom as well as providing speculation about a "holy race."

The Infancy Gospels

There are also two infancy gospels, Infancy James and Infancy Thomas (not to be confused with the Gospel of Thomas) that betray how extensively the myths and legends about the young Jesus and his young mother developed in the second and third centuries.

Neither of these gospels is especially helpful in reconstructing the history of Jesus.

That inventory brings to twenty-three the number of gospels from which data may be extracted for reconstructing a profile of the historical Jesus.

Other Sources

Eusebius (?260–?340) was bishop of Caesarea and confidant of the Emperor Constantine at the Council of Nicea (325 CE). His most important work is his *Ecclesiastical History,* which is the principal source for our knowledge of the history of Christianity from the apostolic age to his own day.

Hegesippus was a Jewish-Christian church historian of the second century CE (precise dates unknown), who wrote five *Books of Memoirs* in opposition to the Gnostics. His works have disappeared, although they are quoted extensively by Eusebius in his *Ecclesiastical History.*

Flavius Josephus (?37–?100) was a Jewish historian who wrote two major histories: *The Jewish War,* which is an account of events leading up to and including the Jewish war with the Romans, 66–73 CE. The second work is called *The Antiquities of the Jews* in twenty books (scrolls), which sketches the history of the Jews from the creation to the beginning of the Jewish war.

Historical Evidence for Jesus of Nazareth beyond Christian Texts

Tacitus, *Annals* 115.44 (112–113 CE)
The "Anointed one," the founder of the name [of the sect], during the rule of Tiberias was put to death by the procurator Pontius Pilate. Restrained for the moment, the deadly superstition broke out again, not only throughout Judea, the origin of the evil, but also through the city in which everything nasty and naughty flows and grows.

Suetonius, *Claudius* 125 (121 CE)
Claudius expelled from Rome Jews who were constantly rioting at the instigation of a certain Chrestus.

***b Sanhedrin* 43a**
On the eve of the Passover Yeshu was hanged. For forty days before the execution took place, a herald went forth and cried, "He is going forth to be stoned because has practiced sorcery and enticed Israel to go astray. Let any one who can say anything in his defense, come and plead on his behalf." But since nothing was brought in his defense he was hanged on the eve of the Passover.

Yeshu had five disciples, Matthai, Nakai, Netzer, Buni and Todah.

Josephus, *Antiquities* 18.63–64 (93–94 CE)
Around this time there was a wise man Jesus, *if one could call him a man*. For he was a performer of

extraordinary deeds, *a teacher of people who take pleasure in the truth.* He won over many Judeans and many from the Greek world. *He was the "Anointed."* Although Pilate, on the indictment of the first men among us, condemned him to the cross, those who loved him from the first did not stop. *For he appeared alive again to them on the third day as the sacred prophets had spoken of these and many other wonders about him.* Even now the clan of the Anointed One, named after him, has not declined.*

*Regular type indicates what most scholars consider historical. The italic may be later Christian insertion.

Reports of the Jesus Seminar

The Complete Gospels. Ed. Robert J. Miller. 4th Edition. Polebridge Press, 2010.

The Complete Gospel Parallels. Eds. Arthur J. Dewey & Robert J. Miller. Polebridge Press, 2012.

> These volumes are indispensible for those interested in the quest. They feature the Scholars Version translation of twenty-three gospels. *The Complete Parallels* allows for an easy comparison of the gospel traditions.

✦

The primary reports of the Jesus Seminar containing color-coded evaluations of all the words and deeds ascribed to Jesus are:

The Five Gospels: The Search for the Authentic Words of Jesus. Robert W. Funk, Roy W. Hoover, and the Jesus Seminar. Macmillan/Polebridge Press, 1993.

> In *The Five Gospels,* the Jesus Seminar examined approximately 1,500 versions of 500 sayings, parables, and dialogues attributed to Jesus. The results of the Seminar's deliberations are reported by colored-coding the texts of all five gospels (Mark, Matthew, Luke, John and Thomas).

The Acts of Jesus: The Search for the Authentic Deeds of Jesus. Robert W. Funk and the Jesus Seminar. HarperSanFrancisco/Polebridge Press, 1998.

> In *The Acts of Jesus,* the Fellows reviewed 387 reports of 176 events reported in all the gospels. They again reported the results of their debates by color-coding all 387 anecdotes.

The Profiles of Jesus. Ed. Roy W. Hoover. Polebridge Press, 2002.

> *The Profiles of Jesus* provides a variety of profiles constructed from the database of sayings and deeds determined to be from the historical Jesus.

The Parables of Jesus: Red Letter Edition. Robert W. Funk, Brandon B. Scott, and James R. Butts. Polebridge Press, 1988.

> *The Parables of Jesus* is a color-coded report on 60 versions of 33 parables attributed to Jesus in a handy 108-page booklet. This was the first public report issued by the Seminar.

Jesus Seminar Guide Series. Ed. Bernard Brandon Scott. Polebridge Press.

1. *Jesus Reconsidered: Scholarship in the Public Eye* (2007)
2. *Listening to the Parables of Jesus* (2007)
3. *Finding the Historical Jesus: Rules of Evidence* (2008)
4. *The Resurrection of Jesus: A Sourcebook* (2008)
5. *Rediscovering the Apostle Paul* (2011)

Designed for classrooms, discussion groups and for the general reader, the Jesus Seminar Guides gather the best writings of Westar Fellows from the pages of its membership magazine, *The Fourth R*, its academic journal, *Forum*, and occasionally from previously unpublished material. Arranged topically, the Guides summarize the important questions and debates that have driven the work of the Jesus Seminar over the last twenty years.

Reimagine the World. Bernard Brandon Scott. Polebridge Press, 2001.

> Scott interprets key parables of Jesus in the context of other things Jesus said and did. The result is a star-

tling and provocative picture of the historical figure and the challenge he presents to contemporary life.

Born Divine. Robert J. Miller. Polebridge Press, 2003.

Robert Miller analyzes the infancy stories of Jesus within the full panoply of ancient birth narratives. The critical consideration of the infancy material enables the reader to detect why the Fellows of the Jesus Seminar regarded the canonical stories as fundamentally mythic.

John the Baptist and Jesus: A Report of the Jesus Seminar. W. Barnes Tatum. Polebridge Press, 1993.

W. Barnes Tatum has provided a concise account of the quest of the historical John the Baptist in this report. The author has sketched the color-coded decisions of the Jesus Seminar along with a lucid analysis of how the Seminar reached its conclusions.

Acts and Christian Beginnings: The Acts Seminar Report. Eds. Dennis E. Smith & Joseph B. Tyson. Polebridge Press, 2013.

The decade long Acts Seminar concluded that Acts dates from the second century. That conclusion directly challenges the view of Acts as history and as the foundational myth of the origins of the Jesus movement thereby raising a host of new questions, addressed in this final report.

Index of Sayings
& Stories

Index of
Ancient Texts

About the Authors

Robert W. Funk (d. 2005) taught at Drew, Vanderbilt, and the University of Montana and served as Annual Professor of the American School of Oriental Research in Jerusalem. A Guggenheim Fellow and Senior Fulbright Scholar, his many books include *The Five Gospels* (1993), *The Acts of Jesus* (1998) and *Honest to Jesus* (1996).

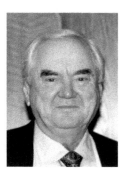

Arthur J. Dewey is Professor of Theology at Xavier University, Cincinnati, Ohio. He is co-author of *The Authentic Letters of Paul* (2010) and *The Complete Gospel Parallels* (2012). For over a dozen years he was a regular commentator on Public Radio Station WVXU in Cincinnati and is a long-time editorial writer for the *Fourth R.*

Lightning Source UK Ltd.
Milton Keynes UK
UKHW022159261021
392889UK00003B/94